HOW TO BUY

AMAZON

MYSTERY BOXES

A COMPREHENSIVE GUIDE TO FINDING VALUE AND HIDDEN TREASURES

MAX TURNER

Published by Max Turner

CONTENTS

INTRODUCTION

In a world where e-commerce reigns supreme, few names evoke more curiosity and excitement than Amazon. This digital marketplace has revolutionized the way we shop, offering everything from everyday necessities to rare collectibles. Among its many offerings, Amazon Mystery Boxes have emerged as a tantalizing phenomenon. These enigmatic packages promise the thrill of the unknown, a treasure trove of surprises waiting to be unveiled. But how does one navigate this intriguing world and come out on top? How can you maximize your chances of scoring big while minimizing risks?

This book is your comprehensive guide to mastering the art of purchasing Amazon Mystery Boxes. Whether you're a seasoned bargain hunter or a curious newbie, you'll find invaluable insights and practical tips to help you make informed decisions. We will delve into the psychology behind the allure of mystery boxes, exploring why the element of surprise captivates us so deeply. You'll learn how to identify reputable sellers, decipher product descriptions, and understand the nuances of box categories to ensure you get the best value for your money.

You'll also discover strategies for managing your expectations and mitigating potential disappointments. After all, not every box will contain a jackpot, but with the right approach, you can enhance your overall experience and increase your chances of finding hidden gems. We'll share real-life success stories and cautionary tales, offering a balanced perspective that will prepare you for the highs and lows of this unique shopping adventure.

Furthermore, we'll explore the ethical and environmental considerations surrounding mystery boxes, helping you make choices that align with your values. From sustainable shopping practices to supporting small businesses, this guide will empower you to make purchases that you can feel good about.

By the end of this book, you'll be equipped with the knowledge and confidence to dive into the world of Amazon Mystery Boxes with a sense of excitement and preparedness. Get ready to uncover secrets, score big, and transform your shopping experience into an exhilarating treasure hunt.

Chapter 1: Introduction to Amazon Mystery Boxes

WHAT ARE AMAZON MYSTERY BOXES?

Imagine a box, sealed with tape, its contents a secret to all but the one who packed it. This is the essence of an Amazon Mystery Box. These unassuming packages are a blend of curiosity and excitement, a modern-day treasure chest that promises the thrill of the unknown.

When you purchase an Amazon Mystery Box, you're engaging in a delightful gamble. The box could contain anything from electronics and gadgets to home decor, fashion accessories, or even rare collectibles. The beauty of these boxes lies in their unpredictability. Unlike conventional shopping where you know exactly what you're getting, a mystery box offers a surprise element that can be both exhilarating and nerve-wracking.

These boxes are typically filled with surplus stock, returned items, or products that need to be cleared out quickly. Retailers and third-party sellers compile these assortments, often categorizing them by general themes such as electronics, toys, or household items. Sometimes, the contents are random, making each box a unique experience.

One might wonder why anyone would choose to buy something without knowing what it is. The answer lies in human nature. People are inherently curious and often seek novelty. The excitement of unboxing something unknown taps into that sense of adventure. There's also the potential for finding a hidden gem, a valuable item that far exceeds the cost of the box itself. This element of risk and reward makes the purchase of mystery boxes akin to a small-scale treasure hunt.

The presentation of these boxes adds to their allure. They arrive at your doorstep, nondescript yet full of potential. The act of opening the box is an event in itself. The anticipation builds as you cut through the tape and peel back the flaps, revealing a glimpse of what's inside. Each item you pull out is a revelation, a piece of the puzzle that was hidden within.

Amazon Mystery Boxes cater to a wide range of interests and budgets. They can be an affordable way to acquire a variety of items, especially for those who enjoy surprises and have a flexible attitude towards what they receive. For some, it's a fun way to try new products without committing to a specific choice. For others, it's a method to obtain items for resale, taking advantage of the bulk nature of these boxes to turn a profit.

There's also a community aspect to consider. Many enthusiasts share their unboxing experiences online, through videos and social media posts. This not only amplifies the excitement but also provides a platform for people to connect over their shared experiences. It's a form of entertainment and community-building that extends beyond the mere act of purchasing.

In essence, Amazon Mystery Boxes are a blend of commerce and entertainment. They offer a break from the predictability of conventional shopping, injecting a bit of spontaneity into the consumer experience. Whether you're a thrill-seeker, a bargain hunter, or just someone looking for a fun diversion, these boxes provide a unique way to engage with the marketplace. The magic lies in the unknown, and the joy is in the discovery.

THE ALLURE OF MYSTERY BOXES

A sense of wonder and anticipation fills the air as one gazes upon the unassuming cardboard box. Its plain exterior, sealed with industrial tape, reveals nothing of the treasures—or trivialities—contained within. The allure of mystery boxes lies in this very enigma, a tantalizing promise of discovery that stirs the imagination and quickens the pulse. Each box, a Pandora's chest, beckons with the potential for delight and surprise.

The human brain is wired to seek novelty and excitement, and mystery boxes tap into this primal urge. The thrill begins the moment the box is ordered, a leap into the unknown that ignites a spark of curiosity. Days of waiting heighten the suspense, each one filled with speculative wonder. What lies beneath the layers of cardboard and packing material? Is it a coveted gadget, a rare collectible, or perhaps something utterly unexpected?

Opening a mystery box is a ritualistic experience, a sensory feast that engages sight, touch, and sound. The ripping of tape, the rustle of packaging, the first glimpse of the contents—all these elements combine to create a moment of pure, unadulterated excitement. The contents are revealed piece by piece, each item adding a new layer to the evolving narrative. Some treasures might evoke a gasp of delight, while others may prompt a puzzled smile. Yet, it is this very unpredictability that makes the experience so intoxicating.

Mystery boxes also offer a unique form of escapism. In an age where much of life is predictable and routine, they provide a portal to a world of endless possibilities. The contents of the box could transport one to distant lands, introduce new hobbies, or simply add a touch of whimsy to the everyday. Each item, whether grand or modest, holds the potential to spark joy and inspire creativity.

The allure is not confined to the contents alone. The entire process, from purchase to unboxing, is a shared experience, often amplified by community engagement. Social media platforms teem with unboxing videos, each one a testament to the shared excitement and communal thrill. Viewers live vicariously through these videos, their anticipation mirroring that of the person unboxing. It is a collective celebration of curiosity, a digital age phenomenon that brings people together in their quest for the unknown.

There is also a certain democratization in the concept of mystery boxes. They offer an accessible form of adventure, one that does not require vast resources or elaborate planning. For a modest sum, anyone can partake in this modern-day treasure hunt, experiencing the same highs and lows, the same moments of wonder and surprise. It is a small investment with the potential for rich emotional returns.

In the end, the true value of a mystery box lies not in the monetary worth of its contents, but in the emotions it evokes. It is a celebration of curiosity, a nod to the childlike wonder that resides within us all. Each box is a reminder that life is filled with mysteries waiting to be uncovered, and that sometimes, the greatest joy comes from the simple act of opening a box and discovering what lies within.

TYPES OF MYSTERY BOXES AVAILABLE

Amazon mystery boxes have become a popular phenomenon, intriguing buyers with the promise of surprise and potential value. These boxes come in various types, each catering to different interests and preferences. Understanding the different types of mystery boxes available can help potential buyers make informed decisions and enhance their unboxing experience.

One of the most common types is the electronics mystery box. These boxes are particularly appealing to tech enthusiasts and gadget lovers. They often contain a mix of items such as headphones, smartwatches, phone accessories, and sometimes even more substantial gadgets like tablets or cameras. The allure of potentially discovering a high-value electronic item at a fraction of its retail price is a significant draw for many buyers.

Fashion and beauty mystery boxes are another popular category. These boxes typically include a range of clothing items, accessories, makeup, and skincare products. For fashionistas and beauty aficionados, the excitement lies in the possibility of uncovering designer brands or trending products. The assortment can vary widely, from everyday essentials to luxury items, making each box a unique treasure trove.

Toys and games mystery boxes cater to both children and the young at heart. These boxes might contain a variety of items, from action figures and dolls to board games and puzzles. For parents, these boxes can be an economical way to surprise their children with new toys, while collectors might find rare or discontinued items that add significant value to their collections.

Book lovers also have their own niche with literary mystery boxes. These boxes typically include a selection of books across various genres, along with related items such as bookmarks, literary-themed accessories, or even exclusive author content. For avid readers, the joy comes not only from the anticipation of new reading material but also from the potential discovery of new favorite authors or genres they might not have explored otherwise.

Home and lifestyle mystery boxes offer a diverse mix of items aimed at enhancing everyday living. These can include kitchen gadgets, home decor, bath products, and other lifestyle accessories. The variety in these boxes makes them ideal for those who enjoy adding new and unique touches to their home environment.

For those with a penchant for collectibles, there are mystery boxes specifically curated with collectible items. These boxes often feature rare or limited-edition items, such as Funko Pop figures, trading cards, and other memorabilia. Collectors appreciate the thrill of potentially finding a rare gem that could significantly increase in value over time.

Health and fitness mystery boxes are designed for the wellness-conscious. They might include items such as workout gear, fitness trackers, supplements, and health-related gadgets. These boxes are perfect for individuals looking to maintain or enhance their fitness routine with new and innovative products.

Additionally, there are niche mystery boxes that cater to specific hobbies or interests. These could range from gardening and DIY crafts to gourmet food and beverages. Each box is carefully curated to provide enthusiasts with new tools, materials, or ingredients to fuel their passion.

In summary, the variety of Amazon mystery boxes available ensures that there is something for everyone. Whether you are a tech geek, fashion lover, bookworm, or fitness fanatic, the thrill of the unknown combined with the potential for high-value discoveries makes these boxes an exciting purchase. Understanding the different types available can help you choose the one that best aligns with your interests and maximizes your unboxing experience.

WHY PEOPLE BUY MYSTERY BOXES

The allure of the unknown has always captivated human imagination. Picture yourself holding a neatly sealed box, its contents shrouded in secrecy. The anticipation builds as you lift the lid, revealing an assortment of items that could range from the mundane to the extraordinary. This thrill, this surge of excitement, is a significant force driving people to purchase Amazon mystery boxes.

Imagine the adrenaline rush as you unwrap the package, your mind racing with possibilities. Will it be a high-tech gadget, a rare collectible, or perhaps an everyday item with an unexpected twist? The element of surprise taps into a primal sense of curiosity, a desire to explore and discover. This anticipation is not just about the physical items inside but also about the emotional journey of discovery.

For some, it's the promise of value that draws them in. The potential to receive products worth far more than the price paid for the mystery box can be irresistible. The prospect of unearthing a hidden gem, an item that surpasses the investment, adds a layer of excitement. This treasure hunt aspect turns the purchase into a game of chance, where the reward could be far greater than the risk.

Others are driven by a sense of nostalgia. The concept of a mystery box can evoke memories of childhood, reminiscent of lucky dips and surprise gifts. It harks back to a time when the simple act of unwrapping a present brought pure joy. This nostalgic pull is powerful, creating a connection between past pleasures and present experiences.

There's also a social aspect to consider. Unboxing videos have surged in popularity on platforms like YouTube and Instagram. People are eager to share their experiences, to showcase the contents of their mystery boxes to an audience. The communal aspect of unboxing, the shared excitement and reactions, creates a sense of belonging and participation in a larger community. It's a way to connect with others through shared curiosity and surprise.

For some, it's about the thrill of the gamble. The uncertainty of what lies inside the box mirrors the unpredictability of life itself. It's a controlled risk, a safe way to experience the highs and lows of chance. This element of unpredictability can be exhilarating, providing a break from the routine and predictable aspects of daily life.

Economically, mystery boxes offer a unique proposition. Retailers often use them as a way to clear out excess inventory, offering consumers a chance to acquire items at a fraction of their usual cost. This can be particularly appealing to bargain hunters, who see the mystery box as an opportunity to score deals on products they might not have otherwise considered.

The diversity of motivations underscores the multifaceted appeal of mystery boxes. Whether driven by curiosity, the search for value, nostalgia, social interaction, or the thrill of the gamble, people find themselves drawn to the enigmatic nature of these boxes. Each purchase is a step into the unknown, a blend of hope, excitement, and anticipation that adds a layer of adventure to the everyday act of shopping.

Chapter 2: Getting Started with Mystery Boxes

CREATING YOUR AMAZON ACCOUNT

Amazon mystery boxes begins with the crucial first step of creating your Amazon account. This process, while straightforward, is the gateway to a treasure trove of possibilities, where hidden gems and surprises await. The initial task is to visit Amazon's homepage, a familiar digital marketplace adorned with a myriad of products and enticing offers. Here, amidst the bustling virtual aisles, lies the small yet significant "Sign In" button, typically positioned at the top right corner of the screen.

Clicking on this gateway reveals two primary options: signing into an existing account or creating a new one. For those new to Amazon, the journey starts by selecting "Create your Amazon account." This action leads to a user-friendly registration page, designed to gather essential information. The form requests a name, email address, and a password. The simplicity of these fields belies their importance, as they form the foundation of your digital identity in the Amazon ecosystem.

Choosing a secure password is paramount. Amazon recommends a mix of uppercase and lowercase letters, numbers, and special characters to fortify your account against potential threats. Once these details are meticulously filled, a verification process ensues. Amazon sends a One-Time Password (OTP) to the provided email address, ensuring that the account creation request is genuine. Retrieving this OTP from your inbox and entering it on the Amazon page completes the verification, solidifying your new account.

With the account now active, the next step is personalizing your profile. This involves adding a delivery address. Navigating to the "Your Addresses" section under the "Your Account" menu allows you to input the location where your mystery boxes will be delivered. Accurate address details are crucial, as they ensure timely and precise delivery of your eagerly anticipated packages. Amazon accommodates multiple addresses, catering to users who might want deliveries at different locations.

Payment information is another critical aspect. Under the "Your Payments" section, you can securely add your preferred payment methods. Credit and debit cards, along with other options like Amazon gift cards, are available to streamline your purchasing process. Amazon employs advanced encryption technologies to safeguard your financial details, ensuring a secure shopping experience.

Exploring the "Account & Lists" menu reveals additional settings to enhance your Amazon experience. Subscription options, order history, and personalized recommendations are just a few of the features at your disposal. Each setting and option is designed to create a seamless, user-friendly environment tailored to your preferences and shopping habits.

The final touch is to familiarize yourself with Amazon's search functionality. The search bar, prominently displayed at the top of the page, is your tool for navigating the vast Amazon marketplace. Typing in keywords related to mystery boxes reveals a plethora of options, each promising a unique and exciting unboxing experience. Filters and sorting options further refine your search, allowing you to zero in on the perfect mystery box that aligns with your interests and budget.

Thus, with your account created and personalized, you stand on the threshold of an exhilarating adventure. The next chapters of this guide will delve deeper into the specifics of purchasing and unboxing Amazon mystery boxes, but for now, your foundation is set, and the world of Amazon is at your fingertips.

NAVIGATING THE AMAZON MARKETPLACE

The vast expanse of the Amazon Marketplace can be both exhilarating and daunting for those seeking the thrill of purchasing mystery boxes. As you step into this digital bazaar, a world of endless possibilities unfolds before you. Every click reveals a new array of tantalizing offers, each box promising an adventure wrapped in cardboard and packing tape.

The first thing to catch your eye is the sheer diversity of sellers. From established brands to individual entrepreneurs, the marketplace is teeming with vendors, each vying for your attention. Their listings are adorned with vibrant images and persuasive descriptions, designed to lure you into their virtual storefronts. It's essential to approach with a discerning eye, as the quality and authenticity of these mystery boxes can vary widely.

Navigating through the categories, you'll find that mystery boxes are often nestled within broader sections like "Toys & Games," "Electronics," and "Collectibles." The titles of these boxes are crafted to ignite curiosity: "Tech Treasure Trove," "Gamer's Paradise," "Vintage Curiosities." Each name is a promise of the unknown, a seductive whisper that there might be something extraordinary hidden inside.

Product reviews become your guiding stars in this expansive marketplace. Reading through them, you'll encounter a mosaic of experiences. Some buyers recount tales of unexpected delight, discovering high-value items far exceeding the cost of the box. Others, however, share cautionary tales of disappointment, receiving items that barely justify the price. Pay close attention to these reviews, especially those that offer detailed accounts and photographs. They provide invaluable insights into what you might realistically expect.

Seller ratings also play a crucial role in your decision-making process. High-rated sellers often have a track record of delivering on their promises, ensuring that the contents of the mystery box align with the description. However, a lower rating doesn't necessarily spell disaster. Sometimes, newer sellers offer great deals to build their reputation. Scrutinize the feedback and weigh the risks and rewards.

As you delve deeper, you'll encounter the allure of limited-time offers and flash sales. These fleeting opportunities can be tempting, but they also require swift, decisive action. Hesitation might mean missing out on a particularly enticing mystery box. However, it's equally important not to rush blindly. Quick decisions should still be informed by research and review checks.

Understanding the return policies of different sellers is another critical aspect. Some vendors offer no returns on mystery boxes, citing the nature of the product. Others might have more flexible terms, allowing returns if the contents are significantly misrepresented. Familiarizing yourself with these policies can save you from potential frustration and financial loss.

Armed with knowledge, you are ready to engage with the Amazon Marketplace more confidently. The thrill of the hunt, the anticipation of the unknown, and the satisfaction of a well-researched purchase all contribute to the unique experience of buying mystery boxes. Each box you choose is a step into an adventure, a small gamble that could yield anything from the mundane to the magnificent.

FINDING REPUTABLE SELLERS

To ensure that the excitement of unboxing these treasures doesn't turn into disappointment, identifying reputable sellers becomes paramount. This crucial step can make the difference between receiving a box filled with delightful surprises and one that leaves you feeling shortchanged.

Begin by delving into seller reviews. Customer feedback is a goldmine of information. Genuine reviews often provide a clear picture of what to expect. Look for sellers who consistently receive high ratings and positive comments. Pay attention to the specifics mentioned in reviews. Comments about the quality of items, the accuracy of descriptions, and the overall satisfaction with the mystery box can guide your decision. Be cautious of sellers with numerous negative reviews or those whose feedback seems too generic or overly positive, as these could be manipulated.

Another effective strategy is to scrutinize the seller's profile. Established sellers often have a detailed profile with comprehensive information about their business. Look for sellers who have been active on Amazon for a considerable period. Longevity often indicates reliability and trustworthiness. A seller with a long history of transactions is likely to be more dependable than a newcomer with little to no track record.

Communication with the seller can also be telling. Reach out with any questions or concerns you might have about the mystery box. A reputable seller will respond promptly and professionally, providing clear and helpful information. Their willingness to engage and assist you is a good indicator of their commitment to customer satisfaction. If a seller is unresponsive or provides vague answers, it might be best to look elsewhere.

Transparency is a hallmark of a trustworthy seller. While the essence of a mystery box is the element of surprise, reputable sellers will still offer some level of detail about what you might find inside. This could include the types of items, the condition they are in, or the general value you can expect. Sellers who are upfront about these aspects demonstrate honesty and a desire to meet customer expectations. Avoid sellers who are overly secretive or make exaggerated claims without providing any substantial information.

Another layer of assurance can be found in the seller's return and refund policies. A reputable seller will have clear and fair policies in place. This not only shows their confidence in the products they offer but also provides you with a safety net should the mystery box not meet your expectations. Carefully read through these policies and ensure you understand the terms before making a purchase.

Engaging with online communities and forums dedicated to Amazon mystery boxes can also be immensely helpful. These platforms are filled with enthusiasts who share their experiences and recommendations. Participating in these discussions can provide you with insights into which sellers are highly regarded and which ones to avoid. The collective wisdom of a community can be a powerful tool in your quest to find reputable sellers.

In your pursuit of the perfect Amazon mystery box, taking the time to find a reputable seller is an investment that pays off in the long run. By leveraging reviews, scrutinizing seller profiles, engaging in clear communication, seeking transparency, understanding return policies, and tapping into community knowledge, you can navigate the marketplace with confidence. The thrill of unboxing a mystery box is unparalleled, and ensuring that you buy from a reputable seller enhances the experience, transforming it into a consistently rewarding adventure.

SETTING A BUDGET

Establishing a clear financial plan is crucial when delving into the world of Amazon mystery boxes. The excitement of potentially uncovering hidden treasures can quickly lead to impulsive decisions if one is not careful. It's essential to approach this venture with a well-defined budget to ensure that the thrill of discovery does not overshadow financial prudence.

Start by assessing your overall financial situation. Take stock of your income, expenses, and any discretionary funds available for leisure activities. This step helps in determining how much money can be comfortably allocated to purchasing mystery boxes without jeopardizing other financial responsibilities. It's important to remember that the contents of these boxes are unpredictable, and while there is potential for profit, there is also a risk of receiving items of little value.

Next, decide on a specific amount that you are willing to spend within a given timeframe. Whether it's a monthly, quarterly, or yearly budget, having a set limit ensures that spending remains controlled. This practice not only helps in managing finances but also adds an element of discipline to the purchasing process. For example, if you allocate $200 a month for mystery boxes, stick to that amount regardless of the temptation to buy more.

Researching the different types of mystery boxes available on Amazon can further refine your budget. Prices can vary significantly, from affordable options costing $20 or less to premium boxes that can go up to several hundred dollars. Understanding the range and average cost of the boxes that interest you allows for better planning and realistic expectations. It might be helpful to start with lower-priced boxes to get a feel for the experience before committing to more expensive options.

Another important aspect to consider is the potential for additional costs. Shipping fees, taxes, and any other hidden charges can add up quickly. Always factor these into your budget to avoid unexpected expenses. Some sellers may offer free shipping or discounts for bulk purchases, so it's worth exploring these options to maximize your budget.

It's also beneficial to set aside a portion of your budget for possible returns or exchanges. While not all sellers offer these options, some do provide a return policy for items that are damaged or significantly not as described. Having a small reserve fund can cover the cost of shipping items back or purchasing replacement boxes if necessary.

Keeping track of your spending is another vital element of budget management. Maintain a record of each purchase, including the cost, contents, and any additional fees incurred. This practice not only helps in staying within the budget but also provides valuable insights into the types of boxes that offer the best value for money. Over time, this data can guide future purchasing decisions, enabling more informed choices and better financial outcomes.

Lastly, regularly reviewing and adjusting your budget is essential. As you gain more experience and understanding of the mystery box market, your financial strategy may need to evolve. Adjusting your budget based on past experiences and current financial circumstances ensures that it remains relevant and effective.

By setting a well-thought-out budget, the excitement of buying Amazon mystery boxes can be enjoyed responsibly. This approach balances the thrill of the unknown with the security of financial stability, making the experience both enjoyable and sustainable.

Chapter 3: Understanding the Risks and Rewards

POTENTIAL RISKS OF BUYING MYSTERY BOXES

Imagine the thrill of receiving a package whose contents are a complete enigma. The anticipation builds as you cut through the tape, the possibilities dancing in your mind. Yet, beneath this excitement lies a labyrinth of potential pitfalls that every buyer must navigate. The allure of Amazon mystery boxes can often overshadow the risks that accompany them, leaving buyers with more than they bargained for.

First and foremost, the contents of these boxes are shrouded in secrecy. What you receive may not match your expectations, and the disparity can be startling. You might envision high-tech gadgets or luxurious accessories, but end up with outdated electronics, unsellable merchandise, or items that are far from valuable. This unpredictability can lead to disappointment, especially when the perceived value of the box does not align with its actual contents.

Moreover, the condition of the items inside the mystery box is another significant concern. Many of these boxes contain returns, overstock, or liquidation items, which means they could be damaged, defective, or missing parts. The excitement of unboxing quickly fades when faced with broken or unusable products. Without any guarantees or the ability to inspect items beforehand, buyers are essentially gambling with their money.

Financial risk is an undeniable factor. The cost of these mystery boxes can vary widely, and the investment might not always pay off. It's possible to spend a considerable amount of money only to find that the items inside are worth far less than what was paid. This discrepancy can be particularly disheartening for those hoping to resell the items for a profit. The anticipated windfall may turn into a financial setback, impacting one's budget and financial goals.

Then, there is the issue of authenticity. In the vast marketplace of Amazon, not all sellers are created equal. Some may include counterfeit or knockoff items in their mystery boxes, passing them off as genuine. This not only undermines the value of the products but also poses ethical and legal dilemmas. Buyers may find themselves unintentionally supporting fraudulent activities or facing complications if they attempt to resell such items.

Customer service and return policies add another layer of complexity. Many sellers of mystery boxes do not offer returns or refunds, leaving buyers stuck with unwanted or faulty items. The lack of recourse can be frustrating and leaves individuals feeling powerless. Unlike traditional purchases where customer satisfaction is often a priority, mystery box transactions can be a one-way street with little room for dispute resolution.

Furthermore, the environmental impact should not be overlooked. The trend of buying mystery boxes contributes to the cycle of consumerism and waste. Unwanted items often end up discarded, adding to landfills and environmental degradation. For those mindful of their ecological footprint, this aspect poses a significant ethical concern.

In the realm of Amazon mystery boxes, the potential risks are as varied as the contents they hold. While the thrill of the unknown can be enticing, it is crucial to approach these purchases with a keen awareness of the possible downsides. The promise of hidden treasures must be weighed against the likelihood of encountering disappointment, financial loss, and ethical quandaries. Buyers must tread carefully, armed with knowledge and a healthy dose of skepticism, to navigate the murky waters of mystery box purchasing.

COMMON REWARDS AND TREASURES

Imagine the thrill of unboxing a treasure chest, each item a potential gem or a rare find. The allure of Amazon Mystery Boxes lies not just in the mystery, but in the tangible rewards and treasures that await inside. As the seal breaks and the box flaps open, the anticipation is palpable, and the possibilities seem endless.

Inside these boxes, one might discover a diverse array of products ranging from everyday essentials to unexpected luxuries. Commonly, you will find electronics, which often include gadgets like headphones, smartwatches, and sometimes even tablets. These items, especially when in good working condition, can offer significant value, making the mystery box purchase feel like a jackpot.

Household items are another frequent inclusion. From kitchen gadgets to décor pieces, these can transform mundane spaces into areas of convenience and style. A high-quality blender or a set of elegant glassware can elevate your home life, making these finds not only useful but also delightful.

Fashion enthusiasts may uncover clothing and accessories that cater to a variety of tastes. From trendy apparel to timeless classics, the range is vast. While there's always a risk that an item might not be to your personal taste, the excitement lies in the potential to discover a new favorite piece or a designer label at a fraction of the cost.

Beauty products are often nestled within these boxes, offering everything from skincare essentials to high-end makeup. The chance to try out new brands or stock up on beloved products can be a major draw for those who love to pamper themselves. Even if a particular shade or scent isn't your preference, these items make great gifts, spreading the joy of discovery to others.

Toys and games frequently appear, making these boxes particularly appealing to families. The delight of finding a popular action figure or an engaging board game can bring joy to children and adults alike. Such treasures not only provide entertainment but also foster family bonding and shared experiences.

Books and media are also common finds. Whether it's a bestselling novel, a classic film on DVD, or a music album, these items can cater to a wide range of interests and hobbies. For avid readers and collectors, discovering a rare edition or a new favorite author can be incredibly rewarding.

While the value and type of items can vary greatly, part of the charm is the element of surprise. The unpredictability can lead to moments of sheer delight when an unexpected treasure is revealed. It's important to approach each unboxing with an open mind, ready to appreciate the serendipitous nature of the experience.

In essence, Amazon Mystery Boxes offer a modern-day treasure hunt, where the rewards are as diverse as they are numerous. Each box is a curated collection of potential delights, waiting to be discovered. Whether it's a practical gadget, a stylish accessory, or a fun toy, the joy of unboxing is amplified by the variety and value of the treasures inside.

BALANCING RISK AND REWARD

The world of Amazon mystery boxes is akin to walking a tightrope, where the thrill of potential treasure must be weighed against the looming possibility of disappointment. Each box is a sealed promise, a Pandora's box that could either shower you with unexpected delights or leave you questioning your decision. The art of balancing risk and reward in this unique marketplace is a delicate dance that requires both intuition and strategy.

Amazon mystery boxes come in various shapes and sizes, each promising an assortment of items that could range from the mundane to the magnificent. The allure lies in the mystery itself; the human brain is wired to seek novelty, and the unknown contents of these boxes tap into that primal curiosity. However, this same curiosity can sometimes cloud judgment, leading to impulsive purchases driven by the thrill of the unknown rather than a calculated assessment of potential value.

To master this balance, one must first understand the types of risks involved. Financial risk is the most obvious; spending money on a box without knowing its contents can be a gamble. There is also the risk of receiving items that are of no personal use or interest, leading to potential waste. Additionally, there is the psychological risk of disappointment, which can be particularly impactful if the anticipation was high.

On the flip side, the rewards can be substantial. Some boxes may contain high-value items that far exceed the purchase price, offering a lucrative return on investment. Others may include rare or unique products that are difficult to find elsewhere, providing a sense of exclusivity and satisfaction. The emotional high of unboxing a treasure trove of unexpected goodies can also be a significant reward in itself, offering a dopamine rush that keeps enthusiasts coming back for more.

To mitigate risks and maximize rewards, a strategic approach is essential. Research is your best ally; understanding the reputation of the seller, reading reviews, and even watching unboxing videos can provide valuable insights into what to expect. Setting a budget and sticking to it can help manage financial risk, ensuring that the thrill of the hunt does not lead to overspending. Diversifying purchases by buying from different sellers or opting for different types of mystery boxes can also spread the risk, increasing the chances of hitting a jackpot.

Another important aspect is managing expectations. Going into the purchase with a realistic mindset can help cushion the blow of potential disappointment. Viewing the purchase as a form of entertainment rather than a guaranteed investment can shift the focus from the material value of the contents to the experience itself. This mindset can transform each unboxing into a fun and exciting event, regardless of the outcome.

Engaging with communities of fellow mystery box enthusiasts can also provide support and guidance. Sharing experiences, tips, and even trading items can enhance the overall experience and provide a sense of camaraderie. These communities often offer a wealth of knowledge and can help newcomers navigate the complexities of the market.

Balancing risk and reward in the world of Amazon mystery boxes is an ongoing process, one that evolves with each purchase and unboxing experience. By approaching it with a blend of curiosity, caution, and strategy, you can turn the act of buying these boxes into a thrilling adventure that offers both excitement and value.

REAL-LIFE SUCCESS STORIES

In the bustling world of e-commerce, the allure of Amazon mystery boxes has captivated countless individuals. Each box, a sealed treasure trove, offers the promise of unexpected delights and potential profit. Stories of those who have ventured into this intriguing realm abound, showcasing both the thrill of discovery and the tangible rewards that can follow.

One such tale belongs to Emily, a young entrepreneur from Seattle. With a modest investment, Emily purchased her first mystery box, filled with a mixture of electronics, toys, and household items. Her keen eye for value allowed her to distinguish between the ordinary and the extraordinary. Among the seemingly mundane contents, she unearthed a high-end smartwatch and a limited-edition action figure. With a few strategic listings on various online marketplaces, Emily swiftly turned her initial investment into a tidy profit. Her success didn't stop there; she reinvested her earnings into more mystery boxes, gradually scaling her small venture into a thriving business.

Then there's the story of Mark, a retired engineer with a passion for gadgets. What began as a hobby quickly transformed into a lucrative side hustle. Mark's analytical skills enabled him to meticulously catalog and evaluate each item he received. His precision paid off when he discovered a rare vintage camera in one of his mystery boxes. The camera, a coveted collector's item, fetched a substantial sum at an online auction. Encouraged by his windfall, Mark continued to delve into the world of mystery boxes, enjoying both the financial gains and the intellectual stimulation of identifying valuable finds.

In another corner of the country, Sarah, a stay-at-home mom from Texas, found an unexpected source of income through Amazon mystery boxes. With a knack for crafts and a flair for marketing, Sarah transformed the items she received into bespoke gift sets. Her creativity shone through in her beautifully curated packages, which she sold through social media platforms. Word of her unique offerings spread, and soon her small enterprise blossomed into a popular online boutique. The mystery boxes provided her not only with products to sell but also with the inspiration to create something truly special.

Each of these stories highlights the diverse ways in which people have harnessed the potential of Amazon mystery boxes. Whether through shrewd resale strategies, niche markets, or creative repurposing, these individuals have demonstrated that with a bit of ingenuity and effort, the contents of a mystery box can be transformed into real value. Their experiences underscore the importance of patience, persistence, and a willingness to explore the unknown.

The excitement of opening a mystery box, the thrill of uncovering hidden treasures, and the satisfaction of turning those finds into profit are universal elements that resonate with anyone who has ever embraced this endeavor. These success stories serve as a testament to the potential that lies within each sealed box, waiting to be discovered by those bold enough to take the plunge.

In the ever-evolving landscape of e-commerce, Amazon mystery boxes continue to offer opportunities for those willing to explore their depths. The stories of Emily, Mark, and Sarah are just a few examples of the countless possibilities that await. Each box holds the promise of adventure, the potential for profit, and the chance to turn the ordinary into the extraordinary.

Chapter 4: Strategies for Buying Mystery Boxes

RESEARCHING BEFORE YOU BUY

The promise of uncovering hidden treasures, coupled with the element of surprise, makes it an enticing adventure for many. However, before plunging headfirst into this venture, it is crucial to arm yourself with adequate knowledge and understanding to ensure a rewarding experience. Conducting thorough research before making a purchase is the cornerstone of this process.

Understanding the concept of Amazon mystery boxes is the first step. These boxes are essentially a collection of items, often returned or overstocked products, bundled together and sold without the buyer knowing the exact contents. The allure lies in the potential for valuable finds at a fraction of their retail price. However, this uncertainty also means that the contents can sometimes be less than desirable. Therefore, a clear comprehension of what you might encounter can help set realistic expectations.

One of the primary aspects to consider is the reputation of the seller. Amazon hosts a plethora of third-party sellers, and their reliability can vary significantly. Delving into reviews and ratings is essential. Previous buyers often leave detailed feedback about their experiences, the quality of the products received, and the accuracy of the seller's descriptions. Paying close attention to these reviews can provide valuable insights and help you avoid potentially unscrupulous sellers.

Another key point is to familiarize yourself with the different types of mystery boxes available. Some sellers specialize in specific categories such as electronics, clothing, toys, or home goods. Identifying your preferences and interests will guide you towards boxes that are more likely to contain items you will find useful or enjoyable. Additionally, some sellers offer themed boxes or those with higher price points that promise premium contents. Understanding these variations can help you make a more informed decision based on your expectations and budget.

It's also important to be aware of the return policies associated with these mystery boxes. Given the nature of these purchases, many sellers may have stringent or non-existent return policies. Carefully reading the terms and conditions can prevent disappointment and ensure you are fully aware of your rights as a buyer. In some cases, even if returns are not accepted, sellers might offer partial refunds or other forms of compensation if the contents are significantly below the advertised value. Knowing these details beforehand can help you navigate any potential issues more smoothly.

Engaging with online communities and forums dedicated to Amazon mystery boxes can also be incredibly beneficial. These platforms are often filled with seasoned buyers who share their experiences, tips, and recommendations. Participating in these discussions can provide a wealth of practical advice and help you stay updated on the latest trends and reputable sellers.

Lastly, setting a budget is a crucial aspect of your research. It's easy to get carried away with the excitement of potentially finding high-value items, but it's important to remain financially prudent. Determine a budget that you are comfortable with and stick to it. This will help you enjoy the experience without any undue financial stress.

In essence, the success of your Amazon mystery box adventure hinges on the diligence of your preliminary research. By taking the time to understand the market, scrutinize sellers, and set realistic expectations, you can embark on this journey with confidence and maximize the enjoyment of uncovering your mystery treasures.

READING REVIEWS AND RATINGS

One of the essential steps in ensuring a rewarding experience is paying close attention to the reviews and ratings provided by previous buyers. These evaluations offer a treasure trove of information, guiding you through the potential pitfalls and hidden gems of the mystery box marketplace.

Imagine the excitement of unboxing a mystery package, the thrill of discovering its contents. However, this excitement can quickly turn to disappointment if the items inside don't meet your expectations. This is where the collective wisdom of the community comes into play. Reviews and ratings serve as a beacon, illuminating the path to a satisfying purchase.

When scanning through reviews, look for patterns. A single negative review might be an outlier, but multiple complaints about the same issue can indicate a recurring problem. Conversely, consistently positive feedback often suggests reliability and quality. Pay attention to the details that reviewers mention. Are they satisfied with the variety and quality of the items? Do they feel they received good value for their money? These insights can help you gauge whether a particular mystery box will meet your expectations.

Some reviewers are more detailed than others, providing comprehensive breakdowns of their unboxing experience. These reviews can be particularly valuable, offering a clear picture of what you might expect. Look for mentions of specific items and their conditions. Are the products new or used? Are they relevant to the advertised theme of the mystery box? Detailed reviews often include photos, which can be incredibly helpful in assessing the quality and variety of the items.

Another crucial aspect to consider is the rating system. Most platforms use a five-star rating scale, with five stars indicating excellent quality and one star indicating poor quality. While it might be tempting to focus solely on the overall rating, it's equally important to read the accompanying comments. A four-star rating with a detailed review explaining minor issues can be more informative than a five-star rating with a brief, generic comment.

Keep an eye out for reviews from verified purchasers. These reviews are generally more trustworthy, as they come from individuals who have genuinely bought and experienced the product. Verified reviews reduce the risk of encountering fake or biased feedback, providing a more accurate picture of what to expect.

It's also beneficial to consider the volume of reviews. A product with hundreds of reviews is likely to give a more reliable overall impression than one with just a handful. However, don't dismiss newer products with fewer reviews outright. Instead, weigh the quality of the feedback available. A few detailed, honest reviews can be more valuable than many vague ones.

In addition to individual reviews, look for trends over time. Has the product maintained consistent quality, or are there indications of a decline? Sometimes, sellers improve their offerings based on feedback, so recent reviews might reflect a better experience than older ones.

Engaging with the community by asking questions can also provide additional insights. Many platforms allow potential buyers to interact with reviewers, clarifying doubts and gathering more information. This interaction not only helps you make an informed decision but also fosters a sense of community among mystery box enthusiasts.

In the realm of Amazon mystery boxes, knowledge is power. By meticulously analyzing reviews and ratings, you can navigate the uncertainties and enhance your chances of a delightful unboxing experience.

TIMING YOUR PURCHASES

Strategically planning the moment you decide to purchase an Amazon mystery box can significantly enhance your chances of uncovering valuable items. Timing is an art in itself, influenced by various factors that can tip the scales in your favor. Imagine the thrill of unboxing a treasure trove of items that could range from the mundane to the extraordinary, all because you chose the optimal time to make your purchase.

One key aspect to consider is the seasonality of shopping trends. During major shopping events like Black Friday, Cyber Monday, and Prime Day, Amazon tends to clear out a substantial amount of inventory. These periods are perfect opportunities to snag a mystery box brimming with high-value items. Retailers often offload excess stock, including high-demand electronics, gadgets, and other coveted items during these sales events. By aligning your purchase with these peak shopping times, you increase the likelihood of scoring big.

Another factor to keep in mind is the end of fiscal quarters. Companies, including Amazon, often push to clear out inventory to make room for new stock and to meet their financial targets. This means that the end of March, June, September, and December can be particularly fruitful times to buy mystery boxes. The pressure to clear out older inventory can result in more valuable items being included in these boxes.

Weekly patterns also play a role. Midweek, particularly Tuesdays and Wednesdays, can be an opportune time to make your purchase. Many consumers tend to shop more on weekends when they have free time, which means that inventory might be more picked over by then. Midweek, however, can offer a refreshed selection of items, increasing your odds of finding something worthwhile.

Personal milestones and special occasions can also influence your timing. Birthdays, anniversaries, or holidays can be great times to treat yourself or someone else to the excitement of a mystery box. The anticipation of receiving a surprise gift adds an extra layer of enjoyment to the experience. Moreover, special occasions often come with promotions and discounts that can make the purchase even more enticing.

Monitoring restock schedules is another strategic move. Amazon often restocks its inventory at specific times, and being aware of these schedules can give you an edge. Early mornings or late nights can be prime times to catch newly listed mystery boxes before they get snapped up by other eager buyers.

It's also worth considering the impact of global events on shopping habits. For instance, during the back-to-school season, you might find mystery boxes loaded with educational supplies, electronics, and other related items. Similarly, post-holiday periods can be a goldmine for discovering leftover holiday stock, ranging from decorations to gifts that didn't quite make it under the tree.

Lastly, staying informed through online forums and social media groups dedicated to mystery box enthusiasts can provide valuable insights. Fellow buyers often share their experiences, including the best times to buy and what types of items they've received during different periods. This collective knowledge can be instrumental in guiding your own purchasing decisions.

In essence, timing your purchase of an Amazon mystery box is about being attuned to the rhythms of retail and leveraging them to your advantage. By considering seasonality, fiscal cycles, weekly patterns, personal milestones, restock schedules, global events, and community insights, you can enhance your chances of uncovering hidden gems. The thrill of the unknown, combined with strategic timing, can turn the simple act of buying a mystery box into an exhilarating treasure hunt.

USING PROMOTIONAL OFFERS AND DISCOUNTS

Promotional offers and discounts hold a unique allure for those venturing into the world of Amazon mystery boxes. These tantalizing deals often serve as the golden tickets to acquiring a plethora of intriguing items at a fraction of their original cost. The savvy shopper knows that timing and strategy are key components in maximizing the benefits of these promotional opportunities.

Amazon, with its vast marketplace, frequently rolls out a variety of promotional offers that can be harnessed to enhance your mystery box purchasing experience. Prime Day, Black Friday, Cyber Monday, and numerous other sales events present a treasure trove of discounted mystery boxes. Each of these events is a beacon for bargain hunters, providing a fertile ground for uncovering hidden gems. Awareness of these sale events and marking them on your calendar is the first step in ensuring you don't miss out on these significant savings.

In addition to the well-publicized sales events, Amazon often provides time-limited lightning deals and daily discounts. These offers are fleeting and require a keen eye and quick action. Subscribing to Amazon's newsletters or enabling notifications on the Amazon app can keep you abreast of these transient deals. The thrill of securing a mystery box at a slashed price is unmatched, but it demands vigilance and promptness.

Another invaluable tool in the arsenal of a mystery box enthusiast is the use of coupon codes. Amazon occasionally issues promotional codes that can be applied at checkout to reduce the price of your purchase. These codes might be found on Amazon's website, through email promotions, or via third-party websites dedicated to aggregating discount codes. Keeping an eye on these sources can result in substantial savings.

Amazon Prime membership is another avenue through which promotional offers can be accessed. Prime members often enjoy exclusive deals and early access to sales events. The annual fee for Prime membership can quickly pay for itself through the savings accrued from these exclusive offers. Furthermore, Prime members benefit from free shipping, which can be particularly advantageous when purchasing heavier or bulkier mystery boxes.

Cashback offers and reward programs also play a significant role in reducing the effective cost of mystery boxes. Utilizing credit cards that offer cashback on purchases or participating in Amazon's own reward programs can lead to additional savings. Accumulated points or cashback can be redeemed on future purchases, effectively lowering the cost of subsequent mystery box acquisitions.

It's also worth exploring third-party sellers on Amazon who offer their own promotional discounts. These sellers often provide competitive pricing and additional discount codes that can be stacked with Amazon's own promotional offers. Reading reviews and checking seller ratings can ensure that you are dealing with reputable vendors, thereby enhancing the overall purchasing experience.

Lastly, bundling purchases can sometimes unlock additional discounts. Sellers may offer reduced prices when multiple items, including mystery boxes, are purchased together. This not only provides a cost-saving opportunity but also amplifies the excitement of uncovering a larger variety of items within the mystery boxes.

The strategic utilization of promotional offers and discounts is an art that can significantly enhance the thrill and value of buying Amazon mystery boxes. By staying informed, acting swiftly, and leveraging the variety of discounts available, one can transform a simple purchase into a rewarding adventure filled with delightful surprises.

Chapter 5: Unboxing and Evaluating Your Finds

THE UNBOXING EXPERIENCE

The moment you receive an Amazon mystery box, anticipation fills the air. The plain cardboard exterior, deceptively mundane, conceals the treasures within. The box's weight, heftier than expected, hints at the myriad of possibilities that lie inside. You run your fingers along the edges, feeling the slight roughness of the corrugated material. The faint aroma of cardboard mingles with the subtle scent of adhesive tape, creating an olfactory prelude to the adventure ahead.

As you prepare to open the box, a sense of excitement courses through you. The act of cutting through the tape, with a sharp knife or a pair of scissors, is a ritual in itself. Each slice through the adhesive barrier is a step closer to unveiling the unknown. The sound of the tape ripping away from the cardboard is oddly satisfying, a prelude to the reveal.

Lifting the flaps of the box, you are greeted by the sight of packing materials. Bubble wrap, packing peanuts, or crumpled paper—each serves as a protective layer, shielding the contents from the rigors of transit. The tactile sensation of pushing aside these materials adds to the suspense. The crinkling noise of the paper or the soft pop of bubble wrap heightens your anticipation.

Your eyes catch the first glimpse of the items inside. They are wrapped in varying layers of plastic, paper, or even fabric, each package a mystery within a mystery. The textures differ—some smooth and sleek, others rough and crinkled. You begin to unwrap the first item, your fingers deftly working through the layers. The process is deliberate, almost meditative, as you peel away each covering.

The first item emerges, and you take a moment to appreciate it. Whether it's a gadget, a piece of clothing, or a quirky trinket, it holds a certain charm. You turn it over in your hands, examining the details. The weight, the texture, the craftsmanship—all contribute to your initial impression. There's a sense of satisfaction in discovering something unexpected, something that you didn't choose but was chosen for you.

You continue to unpack the box, each item revealing itself in turn. Some are instantly recognizable, while others require a moment of contemplation. The variety is part of the allure—no two mystery boxes are ever the same. Each item tells a story, a fragment of the larger narrative that the box represents. You find yourself imagining the journey each product took to reach you, the hands that packed it, the places it has been.

As the last item is unveiled, the box now empty, you take a step back to survey your haul. The mixture of practical items and whimsical curiosities creates a mosaic of experiences. There's a sense of accomplishment, of having navigated the unknown and emerged with newfound treasures. The empty box, once a vessel of mystery, now serves as a reminder of the excitement and joy that the unboxing experience brings.

The process is more than just opening a package; it's an exploration, a discovery, and a moment of connection with the unknown. Each unboxing experience is unique, a testament to the thrill of mystery and the joy of surprise.

ASSESSING THE VALUE OF ITEMS

Opening an Amazon mystery box is akin to unearthing a treasure chest, each item cloaked in the tantalizing veil of the unknown. The allure lies in the potential for high-value finds, but the reality often demands a keen eye and a methodical approach to discern true worth from mere curiosity. The process of assessing the value of items within these enigmatic boxes is both an art and a science, requiring a blend of intuition, research, and practical know-how.

Upon revealing the contents, the initial step is to categorize each item. Grouping by type—electronics, books, clothing, and so forth—provides a structured way to handle the assortment. This organization serves as the foundation for the subsequent valuation process, ensuring no item is overlooked or hastily judged.

For electronics and gadgets, a meticulous examination is paramount. Inspect each device for brand names, model numbers, and condition. Scratches, dents, or missing parts can significantly diminish an item's value. A quick search online for the model number can reveal its market price, but it's crucial to consider the condition. Websites like eBay or Amazon itself offer insights into how much similar items sell for in both new and used conditions. This comparison helps in approximating a realistic resale value.

Books, on the other hand, require a different approach. First editions, signed copies, and out-of-print titles can be particularly valuable. Condition plays a pivotal role—pristine copies with intact dust jackets command higher prices. Online databases such as AbeBooks or even a simple ISBN search can provide a wealth of information regarding a book's current market value. Rare finds might necessitate a deeper dive into specialized forums or contacting a professional appraiser.

Clothing and accessories present another unique challenge. Brand recognition is often the key determinant of value. High-end designer labels or limited-edition pieces can fetch substantial amounts, especially if they are in excellent condition. Tags, original packaging, and authenticity certificates (for luxury items) enhance value significantly. Websites like Poshmark or ThredUp can offer a gauge for resale prices, but remember to factor in wear and tear.

Household items and miscellaneous goods require a broader, yet systematic approach. Vintage items, collectibles, and even quirky novelty products can sometimes be surprisingly valuable. Platforms like Etsy or Craigslist can be useful for gauging interest and potential prices. For items that are less common, niche collector groups or specialized marketplaces might provide the best insight.

Throughout this assessment, documentation is crucial. Photograph each item, note its condition, and record any identifying details such as serial numbers or unique features. This not only aids in valuation but also streamlines the process of listing items for resale, should you choose to do so.

It's important to remain realistic and patient. Not every item will be a hidden gem, and some may hold little to no resale value. However, the cumulative value of multiple lower-priced items can still contribute significantly to the overall worth of the mystery box. Balancing optimism with a pragmatic approach ensures that the experience remains enjoyable and potentially profitable.

In essence, assessing the value of items from an Amazon mystery box is an exercise in diligence and curiosity. Each box offers a unique puzzle, and the satisfaction derived from uncovering a valuable item is matched by the knowledge gained through the process.

HANDLING UNEXPECTED ITEMS

The thrill of unboxing an Amazon mystery box lies in the unknown. With each tear of the packaging, there's a rush of anticipation that courses through your veins. The contents can range from the mundane to the extraordinary, but what truly sets this experience apart is the unexpected items that find their way into your hands. These surprises can be delightful, confusing, or even slightly unsettling. Navigating these unplanned discoveries is an essential skill for any mystery box enthusiast.

When you first encounter an unexpected item, take a moment to assess its condition. Is it brand new, gently used, or obviously worn? This initial inspection can provide clues about its origin and potential value. The excitement of the unknown often leads to hasty conclusions, but a careful, measured approach will ensure that you make the most of every item.

Once you've determined the state of the item, the next step is to identify it. Unmarked objects can be a puzzle in themselves. Utilize your smartphone to conduct a quick image search or consult online forums dedicated to mystery box aficionados. These communities are treasure troves of information and can often help you identify even the most obscure items. The collective knowledge of fellow enthusiasts can turn a perplexing find into a fascinating discovery.

After identifying the item, consider its potential uses. An unexpected item might not fit neatly into your life, but that doesn't mean it lacks value. Think creatively about how it could be repurposed or integrated into your daily routine. For example, a seemingly impractical gadget might turn out to be the perfect solution for a minor inconvenience you hadn't yet addressed. The key is to remain open-minded and flexible.

In some cases, the unexpected item might be better suited to someone else. Re-gifting or trading can be a satisfying way to ensure that these surprises find a loving home. Online marketplaces and local swap meets can be excellent venues for passing on items that don't quite fit your needs. The act of sharing your unexpected finds can also foster a sense of community and camaraderie among fellow enthusiasts.

There will be times when an unexpected item is simply unusable or broken. In these instances, it's important to have a plan for responsible disposal. Recycling or donating parts can minimize waste and give new life to components that would otherwise end up in a landfill. Many communities have specialized recycling programs for electronics, textiles, and other materials, making it easier to dispose of items sustainably.

The unexpected nature of mystery boxes means that not every item will be a hit. However, each surprise presents an opportunity to learn and grow. Handling unexpected items with curiosity and adaptability can enrich your experience and deepen your appreciation for the unpredictable nature of mystery boxes. Every item, whether it becomes a cherished possession or a passing curiosity, contributes to the tapestry of your unboxing adventures.

DOCUMENTING AND SHARING YOUR FINDS

Capturing the excitement of unboxing your Amazon mystery box is a thrilling adventure in itself. As you peel back the layers of packaging, each item you reveal adds a new chapter to your story.

To make the most of this experience, documenting your finds can be both a rewarding and practical endeavor.

Begin by setting the scene. Choose a well-lit area where you can lay out your items and take clear, detailed photos. Natural light is ideal, as it highlights the true colors and textures of your treasures. A clean, uncluttered background ensures that the focus remains on the items themselves. If possible, use a camera with good resolution to capture every nuance, though a smartphone with a decent camera can also do the job.

As you unbox, take note of your initial reactions. Jot down your thoughts in a notebook or use a voice recorder to capture your excitement and impressions in the moment. These spontaneous reactions can add a personal touch to your documentation, making it more engaging and authentic. Pay attention to details such as the condition of the items, any unique features, and your guesses about their potential value.

Organize your finds systematically. Categorize them based on type, size, or any other criteria that make sense to you. This not only helps in keeping track of what you have but also makes it easier to share your discoveries with others. Create an inventory list, including descriptions and any relevant details such as brand names, model numbers, and estimated values.

Sharing your finds can be as enjoyable as discovering them. Social media platforms like Instagram, YouTube, and TikTok are perfect for showcasing your unboxing journey. Create engaging content by combining photos, videos, and your personal commentary. Use hashtags relevant to mystery boxes, unboxing, and Amazon finds to reach a wider audience. Engaging with a community of like-minded enthusiasts can lead to valuable insights, tips, and even potential trades or sales.

For those who prefer a more traditional approach, consider starting a blog or a digital journal. This platform allows you to dive deeper into each unboxing experience, providing detailed reviews and reflections. Include high-quality images and organize your posts by date or theme. A blog can also serve as a comprehensive archive of your mystery box adventures, allowing you to look back and see how your collection has evolved over time.

If you come across items that you don't need or wish to sell, online marketplaces like eBay, Facebook Marketplace, or specialized collector forums can be useful. When listing items for sale, provide clear photos and detailed descriptions to attract potential buyers. Honesty about the condition and any flaws will build trust and increase the likelihood of a successful sale.

Engage with your audience by responding to comments and questions. Share tips and tricks you've learned along the way, and be open to suggestions from others. Building a community around your hobby can enhance the experience, making it more than just about the items but also about the connections and shared enthusiasm.

By documenting and sharing your finds, you not only preserve the excitement of each unboxing but also contribute to a larger community of mystery box enthusiasts. Your journey, marked by each discovery and shared experience, becomes a tapestry of curiosity, surprise, and connection.

Chapter 6: Maximizing Your Profits

RESELLING ITEMS ONLINE

Imagine the thrill of opening a box filled with unknown treasures, each item a potential gem waiting to be discovered. Amazon mystery boxes offer just that—a tantalizing mix of excitement, curiosity, and the promise of hidden value. As you peel back the tape and lift the flaps, a world of reselling opportunities unfurls before your eyes. The contents might range from brand-new electronics to quirky household items, each with its own story and potential for profit.

The key to reselling items from these mystery boxes lies in meticulous organization and sharp instincts. Once the initial excitement of discovering your haul subsides, the real work begins. Each item needs to be carefully examined, cleaned, and assessed for value. This step is crucial; a thorough evaluation can reveal hidden gems that might otherwise be overlooked. Perhaps that seemingly ordinary kitchen gadget is actually a high-demand item on the market, or that obscure-looking figurine is a collector's dream.

Research becomes your trusted ally in this endeavor. Utilize online marketplaces, auction sites, and specialized forums to gauge the current market value of each item. Tools like price comparison websites and historical sales data can provide insights into what buyers are willing to pay. Armed with this knowledge, you can set competitive prices that attract buyers while ensuring a healthy profit margin.

Photographs play a pivotal role in the reselling process. High-quality images can make or break a sale. Clear, well-lit photos that highlight the item's features and condition build trust with potential buyers. Consider taking multiple angles and close-ups of any unique or valuable aspects. A well-composed photo can convey the item's worth far more effectively than words alone.

Crafting compelling product descriptions is equally important. Descriptions should be honest and detailed, providing all the necessary information a buyer might need. Mention the item's condition, any flaws, and its potential uses. Use descriptive language to paint a vivid picture, helping the buyer envision how the item fits into their life. An engaging description not only informs but also entices, sparking the buyer's imagination and desire.

Selecting the right platform to sell your items is another critical decision. Popular options include eBay, Amazon, Etsy, and specialized niche marketplaces. Each platform has its own audience, fees, and selling dynamics. Familiarize yourself with the rules and best practices of each to maximize your success. For instance, eBay's auction-style listings might be ideal for items with uncertain value, while Amazon's Buy Box feature can boost visibility for new products.

Customer service can significantly impact your reselling reputation. Prompt communication, accurate listings, and reliable shipping build trust and encourage repeat business. Handling inquiries and resolving issues professionally can turn a one-time buyer into a loyal customer. Positive reviews and high seller ratings enhance your credibility, attracting more buyers and driving sales.

The art of reselling items from Amazon mystery boxes is a blend of strategy, research, and creativity. Each box is a new adventure, a puzzle waiting to be solved. With diligence and a keen eye for value, you can transform these mysterious assortments into a profitable venture. Whether you're a seasoned seller or a curious newcomer, the world of reselling offers endless possibilities and the thrill of the unknown.

UTILIZING SOCIAL MEDIA PLATFORMS

When diving into the world of Amazon mystery boxes, social media platforms become invaluable tools for both research and community engagement. These platforms provide real-time insights and a plethora of opinions that can guide your purchasing decisions. The first step involves identifying which platforms are most frequented by enthusiasts and sellers of Amazon mystery boxes. Typically, Facebook, Instagram, YouTube, and Reddit serve as the primary hubs for this niche market.

On Facebook, numerous groups and pages are dedicated to the discussion and trading of Amazon mystery boxes. By joining these groups, you gain access to a wealth of user-generated content, including unboxing videos, reviews, and tips from seasoned buyers. Engaging with these communities allows you to ask questions, share your experiences, and even spot potential scams. The interactive nature of Facebook groups fosters a sense of camaraderie, where members are often willing to share their knowledge and help newcomers navigate the complexities of buying mystery boxes.

Instagram, with its visual-centric approach, offers a different yet equally valuable perspective. Influencers and everyday users alike post unboxing videos and photos, often accompanied by detailed captions that describe their experiences. By following hashtags like #AmazonMysteryBox or #MysteryBoxUnboxing, you can discover a plethora of posts that provide a visual representation of what to expect. Instagram Stories and IGTV also serve as platforms where users share live or recorded unboxings, giving you an authentic look at the contents and quality of various mystery boxes.

YouTube stands out as a treasure trove of information, thanks to its extensive library of unboxing videos. Channels dedicated to mystery boxes often provide comprehensive reviews and comparisons, showcasing the highs and lows of different sellers and boxes. Watching these videos helps you gauge the consistency and reliability of specific sellers, and the comment sections often contain additional insights from viewers. Subscribing to these channels ensures you stay updated on the latest trends and releases, making YouTube an essential resource for any mystery box enthusiast.

Reddit offers a more text-based, community-driven experience. Subreddits like r/MysteryBoxes and r/AmazonDeals are filled with discussions, reviews, and advice from fellow buyers. The anonymity of Reddit encourages honest and unfiltered opinions, making it a trustworthy source for gauging the reputation of various sellers. Participating in these discussions not only enhances your knowledge but also connects you with a network of like-minded individuals who share your interest.

Each social media platform brings its unique strengths to the table, and utilizing a combination of them ensures a well-rounded approach to buying Amazon mystery boxes. By actively engaging with these platforms, you can stay informed about the latest trends, avoid common pitfalls, and make more informed decisions. Whether you're a novice or an experienced buyer, leveraging social media enhances your overall experience, making the journey of purchasing Amazon mystery boxes both exciting and rewarding.

JOINING MYSTERY BOX COMMUNITIES

Diving into the world of Amazon mystery boxes can be an exhilarating experience, but one of the most rewarding aspects of this adventure is connecting with like-minded individuals. These communities are vibrant ecosystems where enthusiasts share their discoveries, offer advice, and celebrate the thrill of the unknown together. Picture a bustling marketplace, where excitement is palpable, and every conversation brims with anticipation and curiosity.

The first step in finding these communities is to explore social media platforms such as Facebook, Reddit, and Instagram. On Facebook, groups dedicated to mystery box unboxings can be treasure troves of information. Members frequently post their latest finds, ranging from rare collectibles to everyday items with surprising value. The atmosphere in these groups is often welcoming and inclusive, encouraging both newbies and seasoned unboxers to participate. Engaging in these groups can provide invaluable insights, from identifying reputable sellers to learning about the best times to make purchases.

Reddit, with its vast array of specialized subreddits, is another excellent resource. Subreddits like r/MysteryBox and r/Unboxing are bustling hubs where users share detailed reviews, unboxing videos, and even cautionary tales. The beauty of Reddit lies in its upvote system, which helps highlight the most useful and popular posts. This democratic approach ensures that the community's collective wisdom is easily accessible. Engaging in discussions, asking questions, and sharing your own experiences can help build your reputation within the community and foster deeper connections with fellow enthusiasts.

Instagram offers a more visual approach to the mystery box phenomenon. By searching hashtags like #mysterybox and #unboxing, you can find countless posts showcasing the latest hauls. Influencers and everyday users alike share their unboxing experiences through photos and videos, often accompanied by detailed captions and reviews. Following popular accounts and engaging with their content can not only provide inspiration but also keep you informed about trends and reputable sellers. The visual nature of Instagram makes it a perfect platform for those who enjoy seeing the tangible excitement of unboxing.

Participating in these communities also means staying informed about upcoming sales, exclusive deals, and limited-edition boxes. Many sellers and retailers announce special promotions through these channels, giving community members a first look at what's available. Being active in these groups can sometimes grant you access to early-bird discounts or insider information that isn't available to the general public.

Moreover, these communities are excellent places to learn about the pitfalls and challenges associated with buying mystery boxes. Members often share their disappointments and mistakes, offering cautionary advice to help others avoid the same issues. This collective knowledge can be invaluable, especially for newcomers who are still learning the ropes. From spotting counterfeit products to understanding return policies, the shared experiences of the community can guide you in making informed decisions.

Connecting with mystery box communities is more than just a way to enhance your unboxing adventures; it's about becoming part of a shared experience. The camaraderie, the shared excitement, and the wealth of knowledge available can significantly enrich your journey. Whether you're seeking advice, looking for the latest deals, or simply wanting to share your own unboxing stories, these communities offer a supportive and enthusiastic environment that celebrates the joy of discovery.

TRACKING YOUR EARNINGS

Keeping a close eye on your earnings is essential when diving into the world of Amazon mystery boxes. Each box holds potential surprises, and while the thrill of discovery is a significant part of the appeal, understanding the financial side is crucial for long-term success. The first step in tracking your earnings is to maintain a detailed log of every purchase you make. Record the cost of each mystery box, including any shipping fees or additional expenses incurred. This foundational data will serve as the baseline for evaluating your investments.

Once you have your costs documented, the next step is to record the contents of each box meticulously. List every item, noting its condition, brand, and any other relevant details. This will help you assess the potential resale value. Utilize online marketplaces like eBay or Amazon itself to check the current selling prices for similar items. This research will provide a realistic estimate of what you can expect to earn from each item.

After estimating the value of the items, it's time to calculate your potential profit. Subtract the total cost of the mystery box from the estimated resale value of its contents. This will give you a clear picture of your earnings from each purchase. It's important to remember that not every box will yield a profit. Some may contain items of little value, while others might surprise you with high-ticket goods. The key is to look at the overall trend rather than individual boxes.

Consistency in recording and reviewing your earnings is vital. Set aside time regularly to update your earnings log, ideally after each unboxing session. This habit will help you stay organized and make informed decisions about future purchases. Additionally, tracking your earnings over time will reveal patterns and trends, enabling you to refine your buying strategy. For instance, you might notice that boxes from certain sellers or categories consistently yield higher profits.

Another important aspect of tracking your earnings is to consider the time and effort involved in reselling the items. Factor in the time spent on photographing, listing, and shipping each item. This will give you a more accurate picture of your net earnings and help you determine if the endeavor is worth your time. Efficiency in these processes can significantly impact your overall profitability.

Utilize tools and apps designed for resellers to streamline the tracking process. There are various inventory management systems available that can help you keep track of your items, sales, and profits. These tools often come with features like automated pricing suggestions, sales tracking, and even integrated shipping solutions, making it easier to manage your reselling business.

Networking with other mystery box enthusiasts can also provide valuable insights. Join online forums, social media groups, or local reseller communities to share experiences and tips. Learning from others can help you avoid common pitfalls and discover new strategies for maximizing your earnings.

Remember, the goal is to enjoy the process while also making a profit. By diligently tracking your earnings and staying organized, you can turn the excitement of unboxing Amazon mystery boxes into a rewarding and profitable venture. Each box is a learning experience, and with careful tracking, you can continually improve your approach and increase your chances of success.

Chapter 7: Avoiding Scams and Pitfalls

IDENTIFYING RED FLAGS

Amazon mystery boxes can be thrilling, with the promise of unexpected treasures awaiting inside each package. However, this excitement can sometimes cloud our judgment, making it crucial to recognize potential pitfalls before making a purchase. The first and most vital step in this journey is to identify the red flags that could indicate a less-than-ideal buying experience.

One of the most telling signs is the seller's reputation. A reputable seller will have a history of positive reviews and satisfied customers. Take the time to read through reviews and ratings, paying close attention to recurring themes. Are previous buyers frequently delighted with their purchases, or do they often express disappointment? Look for detailed feedback that mentions the quality and value of the items received. A pattern of negative reviews, especially those highlighting issues such as missing items, poor quality, or misleading descriptions, should be a significant warning sign.

Another critical aspect to consider is the transparency of the listing. Sellers who provide clear, honest descriptions and set realistic expectations are typically more trustworthy. Be wary of listings that are overly vague or make grandiose claims without any substantiation. For example, a mystery box described as containing "high-value electronics" without any further details or assurances might be too good to be true. Authentic sellers will often include information about the types of items that could be included, their condition, and any warranty or return policies.

Price is another factor that can reveal much about the legitimacy of a mystery box. While it's natural to be drawn to a good deal, prices that seem unusually low compared to the promised contents should raise a red flag. A seller offering a box full of premium electronics for a fraction of their retail price might be cutting corners somewhere, whether in the quality of the items or the accuracy of their descriptions. It's essential to strike a balance between a reasonable price and the value you're expecting to receive.

Additionally, consider the seller's communication. Reliable sellers are typically responsive and willing to answer any questions you might have about the mystery box. If a seller is evasive, slow to respond, or provides vague answers, it could indicate a lack of professionalism or even an attempt to hide something about the product. Clear, open communication is a hallmark of a trustworthy seller and can provide peace of mind as you make your purchase.

Shipping and handling practices also offer insight into the seller's reliability. A reputable seller will provide detailed shipping information, including tracking numbers and estimated delivery times. Pay attention to the shipping costs as well; exorbitant fees can sometimes be a tactic to offset a low listing price, ultimately making the deal less favorable. Ensure that the seller has a clear return policy in place, allowing you to return the box if it doesn't meet your expectations.

Lastly, consider the overall presentation of the seller's online presence. Professionalism in their listings, website, and customer interactions can reflect their commitment to providing a good buying experience. Poorly written descriptions, low-quality images, and a lack of coherent branding may indicate a less reliable seller.

By carefully evaluating these aspects, you can mitigate the risks associated with buying Amazon mystery boxes and increase your chances of a satisfying and exciting purchase.

DEALING WITH FRAUDULENT SELLERS

Mystery boxes can be filled with the promise of unexpected treasures and delightful surprises. However, amidst the excitement, it's essential to remain vigilant and discerning to avoid falling prey to fraudulent sellers. These unscrupulous individuals can tarnish the experience, leading to disappointment and financial loss. To safeguard your investment and ensure a positive experience, several key strategies and considerations can be employed.

Understanding the nature of fraudulent sellers is the first step. These sellers often lure buyers with enticing deals, flashy advertisements, and too-good-to-be-true promises. They might use high-quality photos of mystery boxes brimming with valuable items, only to deliver boxes filled with worthless trinkets or, in some cases, nothing at all. Recognizing these red flags early on can save both money and frustration.

One effective strategy is to thoroughly research the seller before making a purchase. Examining the seller's ratings and reviews on Amazon can provide valuable insights into their legitimacy. Genuine sellers typically have a trail of positive feedback and satisfied customers. Conversely, fraudulent sellers often have numerous negative reviews, with complaints about misleading descriptions, poor customer service, and subpar products. It's wise to read through these reviews carefully, paying attention to recurring issues or patterns of deception.

Another crucial aspect is communication. Reputable sellers are usually responsive and transparent, willing to answer questions and provide additional information about their mystery boxes. Engaging in a conversation with the seller can help gauge their credibility. If a seller is evasive, unresponsive, or reluctant to provide details, it might be a sign to proceed with caution or avoid the transaction altogether.

Payment methods also play a significant role in protecting against fraud. Utilizing secure payment options like credit cards or Amazon Pay can offer an extra layer of security. These methods often come with buyer protection policies, allowing for disputes and chargebacks in cases of fraudulent activity. Avoiding direct bank transfers or unconventional payment methods can reduce the risk of losing money to a scam.

Additionally, setting realistic expectations is vital. While the allure of finding high-value items in a mystery box is strong, it's essential to remember that these boxes are, by nature, a gamble. Approaching the purchase with a sense of adventure rather than a guaranteed profit can help mitigate disappointment. Recognizing that not every box will contain a jackpot can lead to a more enjoyable and less stressful experience.

In the unfortunate event of encountering a fraudulent seller, taking swift action is crucial. Reporting the seller to Amazon can help protect other buyers and potentially lead to a resolution for your case. Documenting all communications and transactions can provide evidence if a dispute arises. Amazon's customer service can be a valuable ally in resolving issues and seeking refunds.

By staying informed, conducting thorough research, and maintaining a cautious approach, the risks associated with fraudulent sellers can be significantly minimized. Embracing these strategies ensures that the thrill of unboxing Amazon mystery boxes remains a joyful and rewarding experience, free from the pitfalls of deception and disappointment.

PROTECTING YOUR PERSONAL INFORMATION

The thrill of unboxing the unknown can be exhilarating, but beneath that excitement lies a crucial consideration: safeguarding your personal information. Navigating this digital landscape requires a keen awareness of the potential risks and a proactive approach to protecting oneself.

When you decide to purchase an Amazon mystery box, the first step is to ensure that the seller is reputable. Scour the reviews, both positive and negative, to gauge the experiences of previous buyers. A trustworthy seller will have a pattern of satisfied customers and transparent practices. Be wary of sellers with sparse feedback or those who have recently emerged on the platform; their lack of history can be a red flag.

Once you've found a credible seller, the next stage involves the transaction itself. This is where your personal information comes into play. It's essential to use a secure payment method, such as a credit card or a trusted third-party payment service. These options often provide additional layers of protection and recourse in case of fraudulent activity. Avoid using direct bank transfers or unfamiliar payment platforms, as these can leave you vulnerable to scams.

Another critical aspect is the information you share during the purchase process. Limit the details you provide to only what is necessary. Be cautious of sellers who request excessive personal data, such as your social security number or detailed bank account information. Such requests are uncommon and should raise immediate suspicion. Always verify the legitimacy of the seller's website or online store before inputting any sensitive information.

Equally important is the protection of your data post-purchase. Once your mystery box is on its way, monitor your financial statements and online accounts for any unusual activity. Cybercriminals often strike when least expected, and early detection can prevent significant damage. Utilize alerts and notifications offered by your bank or payment service to stay informed of any transactions made with your account.

To further shield your personal information, consider the use of virtual private networks (VPNs) when shopping online. A VPN can encrypt your internet connection, making it more difficult for hackers to intercept your data. This is particularly useful when accessing public or unsecured Wi-Fi networks, which are common hotspots for cyberattacks.

Additionally, be mindful of phishing attempts. Cybercriminals often send deceptive emails or messages that appear to be from legitimate sources, such as Amazon or your bank. These communications may urge you to click on a link or provide personal information. Scrutinize the sender's address, look for grammatical errors, and avoid clicking on suspicious links. When in doubt, contact the company directly through their official channels to verify the authenticity of the message.

In the realm of online shopping, knowledge is power. Educate yourself about the latest cybersecurity threats and follow best practices to safeguard your personal information. Regularly update your passwords, using complex combinations of letters, numbers, and symbols. Enable two-factor authentication wherever possible to add an extra layer of security to your accounts.

The excitement of purchasing an Amazon mystery box should not come at the cost of your personal security. By taking these precautions, you can enjoy the thrill of the unknown with peace of mind, knowing that your personal information is well-protected.

REPORTING SCAMS TO AMAZON

However, as with any online marketplace, it's important to remain vigilant and aware of potential scams. If you find yourself in a situation where you suspect foul play, knowing how to report scams to Amazon is crucial.

Begin by gathering all pertinent information related to the transaction. This includes order numbers, seller details, product descriptions, and any correspondence you may have had with the seller. Documentation is key in presenting a clear and compelling case to Amazon's support team. Screenshots of product listings and communication threads can provide concrete evidence to support your claim.

Next, navigate to Amazon's customer service portal. This can typically be found by scrolling to the bottom of Amazon's homepage and selecting the "Help" link. From there, you will be directed to a page with various support options. Select the option that most closely aligns with your issue, which in this case would be something related to a fraudulent transaction or a problem with your order.

Amazon offers multiple methods for contacting their support team, including live chat, email, and phone support. While live chat and phone support can offer immediate assistance, email might be preferable if you need to provide detailed information and attach supporting documents. When contacting support, be concise yet thorough in explaining your situation. Clearly state that you believe you have been scammed, and provide all the gathered evidence to substantiate your claim.

Amazon takes fraud very seriously, and their support team is trained to handle such issues with diligence. They will likely initiate an investigation into the matter, which may involve reviewing the seller's history, the transaction details, and the evidence you've provided. During this period, it's important to remain patient and cooperative, as investigations can take time to ensure a thorough review.

While the investigation is ongoing, continue to monitor your email for updates from Amazon. They may require additional information or clarification to proceed with their inquiry. Providing timely and accurate responses can help expedite the process. In some cases, Amazon may decide to refund your purchase or take corrective action against the seller to prevent future incidents.

It's also beneficial to leave a detailed review of your experience on the seller's profile. This serves as a warning to other potential buyers and contributes to the overall integrity of the marketplace. Be factual and avoid emotional language, as this will make your review more credible and impactful.

Protecting yourself from scams is an ongoing process. Regularly reviewing Amazon's guidelines on safe buying practices, staying informed about common scam tactics, and exercising caution with unfamiliar sellers can significantly reduce the risk of encountering fraudulent activities. By reporting scams and sharing your experiences, you contribute to a safer, more reliable shopping environment for everyone.

In the ever-evolving landscape of online shopping, staying vigilant and proactive is your best defense against scams. By understanding the appropriate channels and methods for reporting fraudulent activities to Amazon, you not only protect yourself but also help maintain the integrity of the marketplace.

Chapter 8: Advanced Tips and Tricks

LEVERAGING DATA AND ANALYTICS

Understanding the intricacies behind purchasing Amazon mystery boxes requires a methodical approach. By leveraging data and analytics, one can transform what appears to be a gamble into a calculated decision. This process begins with gathering as much information as possible on the different types of mystery boxes available. Each box, often categorized by themes such as electronics, toys, fashion, or general merchandise, presents a unique set of probabilities and potential returns.

The first step involves data collection from previous purchases. Online forums, review sites, and social media platforms are rich sources of user experiences and insights. By compiling data from these sources, patterns start to emerge. For instance, certain themes might consistently offer higher value items, while others might have a higher frequency of lower-value goods. Analyzing this data helps in identifying which categories have historically provided the best returns on investment.

Once the data is collected, it's crucial to analyze it using statistical tools and software. Basic statistical methods such as mean, median, and mode can offer insights into the average value of items received in different types of boxes. More advanced techniques like regression analysis can help in understanding the relationship between the cost of the box and the average value of its contents. By employing these methods, one can predict the potential value of a mystery box before making a purchase.

Another important aspect is understanding the seller's reputation. Data analytics can be employed to track the performance and reliability of different sellers offering mystery boxes. By analyzing customer feedback and ratings over time, trends can be identified. Sellers with consistently high ratings and positive feedback are more likely to offer boxes with valuable items. On the other hand, sellers with fluctuating ratings or frequent complaints might be a higher risk.

Price tracking tools and historical price data can also be beneficial. These tools allow buyers to monitor the price changes of mystery boxes over time. By analyzing this data, one can identify the best times to purchase a box, potentially taking advantage of price drops or promotional periods. Historical data analysis can also reveal if certain times of the year yield better box contents, such as during holidays or major sales events.

Leveraging machine learning algorithms can further enhance the decision-making process. Algorithms can be trained to predict the potential value of a mystery box based on historical data, seller reputation, and current market trends. These predictive models can offer recommendations on whether a particular box is worth purchasing or not. By continuously feeding new data into these models, their accuracy and reliability improve over time.

In addition to quantitative data, qualitative insights are equally important. Sentiment analysis on customer reviews can provide a deeper understanding of the general satisfaction level with different types of mystery boxes. This analysis can reveal whether customers feel they are getting their money's worth or if there are common complaints about certain boxes or sellers.

By systematically leveraging data and analytics, purchasing Amazon mystery boxes can become a more informed and strategic activity. This approach minimizes the risks associated with the inherent uncertainty of mystery boxes and maximizes the potential for discovering valuable items.

BUILDING RELATIONSHIPS WITH SELLERS

Establishing a successful venture into the world of Amazon mystery boxes hinges on more than just luck and curiosity. A significant part of the process involves forging strong relationships with sellers. These relationships can be the key to unlocking the best deals, gaining insider information, and ensuring a steady supply of intriguing boxes.

First and foremost, communication is the cornerstone of any good relationship. When reaching out to sellers, it's essential to be clear and respectful. Introduce yourself politely and express genuine interest in their products. Sellers are more likely to respond positively to buyers who show respect for their time and business. A well-crafted message can set the tone for future interactions, paving the way for a mutually beneficial relationship.

Regular communication helps build trust. Follow up with sellers after making a purchase to provide feedback. Whether the feedback is positive or constructive, sellers appreciate buyers who take the time to share their experiences. This not only demonstrates your engagement but also shows that you value their efforts. Over time, this can lead to sellers prioritizing you when they have new or exclusive mystery boxes available.

Attending to detail is another crucial aspect. Sellers often have a wealth of information in their listings, and taking the time to read through these details can provide valuable insights. By understanding their terms, conditions, and the nature of their offerings, you can tailor your approach and inquiries more effectively. This demonstrates your seriousness and can differentiate you from less attentive buyers.

While it's important to be professional, a touch of personal connection can go a long way. Sharing a bit about your own interests and what draws you to mystery boxes can create a more relatable and memorable interaction. Sellers, like any business people, appreciate knowing their buyers on a slightly more personal level. This doesn't mean oversharing but rather finding common ground or expressing genuine enthusiasm for their products.

Flexibility and patience are virtues in this realm. Sellers often operate under various constraints, whether it's limited stock, shipping delays, or other logistical challenges. Being understanding and accommodating can strengthen your relationship. If a seller knows that you are a reliable and patient buyer, they are more likely to go the extra mile for you in the future.

Another practical tip is to support sellers through social media and reviews. Many sellers have social media profiles or depend on reviews to build their reputation. Following them, engaging with their posts, and leaving thoughtful reviews can significantly boost their business. This kind of support does not go unnoticed and can make you a preferred customer.

Moreover, repeat business is a powerful tool. Regularly purchasing from the same sellers can lead to better deals and exclusive offers. Sellers appreciate loyal customers and are often willing to offer discounts or early access to new mystery boxes as a token of appreciation.

Lastly, always approach negotiations with a win-win mindset. While it's natural to seek the best deal, remember that sellers are running a business. Fair negotiations where both parties feel satisfied can lead to long-term relationships and more fruitful exchanges. By showing that you value the seller's time and effort, you are more likely to secure ongoing benefits.

Building relationships with sellers requires effort, patience, and a genuine interest in their products and business. These connections can transform your experience with Amazon mystery boxes from a casual hobby into a rewarding and sustainable venture.

EXPLORING NICHE MYSTERY BOXES

With a world of endless possibilities contained within, niche mystery boxes offer a unique and thrilling experience for the discerning adventurer. Unlike their more general counterparts, these boxes are curated with a specific theme or interest in mind, catering to a particular passion or hobby. The allure of these boxes lies in their ability to both surprise and delight, presenting an array of items that resonate deeply with the recipient's personal tastes.

Imagine receiving a box devoted entirely to vintage comic books. The anticipation builds as you carefully slice through the packaging tape, revealing a treasure trove of nostalgic delights. Each comic, carefully selected for its rarity or historical significance, tells a story not just on its pages but through its very existence. The scent of aged paper and the vivid colors of the covers transport you back to the golden age of superheroes, where every issue was a portal to another world.

For those with a culinary inclination, a gourmet food mystery box might be the perfect indulgence. Opening such a box could reveal an assortment of exotic spices, artisanal cheeses, or rare chocolates. Each item invites you to embark on a gastronomic adventure, exploring flavors and textures that might be new and exciting. The enclosed recipe cards or pairing suggestions add an educational element, transforming the experience from mere consumption to a journey of culinary discovery.

The world of beauty and skincare enthusiasts is another realm ripe for exploration. A mystery box filled with high-end skincare products, luxurious face masks, and innovative beauty tools can feel like a spa day in a box. The tactile pleasure of unwrapping each item, the anticipation of trying new products, and the joy of discovering a new favorite make this type of box a self-care ritual in itself.

For the tech-savvy, a gadget-themed mystery box offers a different kind of thrill. Each box might contain anything from the latest smart home devices to quirky, innovative tools that solve everyday problems in unexpected ways. The excitement here lies in the potential for discovery and the promise of integrating new technology into your daily life, enhancing your routines and possibly even transforming them.

Collectors, too, find a special allure in niche mystery boxes tailored to their specific interests. Whether it's rare coins, limited-edition action figures, or vintage vinyl records, each box is a curated experience, a small museum of wonders that speaks directly to the collector's heart. The joy of adding a rare find to your collection, or discovering an item you never knew existed, is a unique thrill that only a well-curated mystery box can provide.

Craft enthusiasts might find their perfect match in a box filled with DIY kits, unique materials, and crafting tools. Each item within serves as a spark for creativity, encouraging you to start new projects and explore different techniques. The satisfaction of completing a project and the pride in creating something with your own hands are unparalleled rewards.

Niche mystery boxes are not just about the items they contain; they are about the experience they provide. The anticipation, the discovery, and the personal connection to the contents make each box a small adventure. They offer a way to indulge in your passions, explore new interests, and find joy in the unexpected.

STAYING UPDATED WITH MARKET TRENDS

Being successful in this unique marketplace demands a continuous effort to stay updated with the latest market trends. This dynamic environment is influenced by a myriad of factors, including seasonal shifts, consumer behavior, and emerging product categories. By staying informed, you can make more strategic purchasing decisions and potentially uncover hidden gems that others might overlook.

One of the primary ways to stay current is by leveraging online resources. Websites and forums dedicated to reselling and unboxing can provide invaluable insights. These platforms often feature detailed discussions about recent trends, popular items, and tips from seasoned buyers. Engaging with these communities not only keeps you informed but also allows you to share your own experiences and learn from others.

Social media is another powerful tool for tracking market trends. Platforms like Instagram, YouTube, and TikTok are brimming with influencers and enthusiasts who regularly post unboxing videos and reviews of mystery boxes. Following these accounts can give you a real-time glimpse into what's trending and what's not. Pay attention to the types of products that generate the most excitement and engagement, as these are likely to be in high demand.

E-commerce analytics tools can also be instrumental in staying updated. These tools can provide data on best-selling items, price fluctuations, and consumer preferences. By analyzing this data, you can identify patterns and predict which types of products are likely to be popular in upcoming mystery boxes. This information can help you make more informed decisions about which boxes to purchase and when.

Seasonal trends play a significant role in the types of products available in Amazon mystery boxes. For example, around the holiday season, you might find a higher proportion of toys, electronics, and festive decorations. Conversely, during back-to-school periods, there may be an influx of stationery, backpacks, and educational supplies. Being aware of these seasonal shifts can help you time your purchases to align with your interests or resale strategies.

Consumer behavior is another crucial factor to consider. Trends can change rapidly based on cultural events, technological advancements, and even viral social media challenges. For instance, a sudden surge in popularity for a particular gadget or fashion item can lead to an increased presence of these products in mystery boxes. Keeping an eye on consumer trends can give you a competitive edge in identifying valuable items.

Networking with other buyers and sellers can provide additional insights into market trends. Building relationships with others in the community can lead to the exchange of tips and information that you might not find elsewhere. Attending trade shows, reselling events, and online webinars can also expose you to new trends and opportunities.

Staying updated with market trends is not just about gathering information but also about being proactive in applying that knowledge. Regularly reviewing your past purchases and their outcomes can help you refine your strategy. Identify which types of boxes yielded the most valuable items and which ones fell short of expectations. This self-assessment can guide your future decisions and improve your overall success rate.

In this ever-evolving marketplace, staying informed is your best defense against uncertainty and your greatest asset in uncovering the true potential of Amazon mystery boxes.

Chapter 9: Legal and Ethical Considerations

UNDERSTANDING AMAZON'S POLICIES

Amazon's policies form the bedrock of any purchasing decision, especially when it comes to the intriguing world of mystery boxes. These policies are essential to grasp, as they outline the rules, regulations, and guidelines that govern transactions on the platform. Understanding these policies can make the difference between a satisfying purchase and a frustrating experience.

Amazon has a comprehensive set of policies designed to protect both buyers and sellers. These policies cover a wide range of topics, from payment methods to return procedures, and even the types of products that can be sold on the platform. For someone interested in buying mystery boxes, these policies are particularly relevant, as they can affect everything from what you receive to how you handle disputes.

One of the most critical policies to understand is Amazon's A-to-Z Guarantee. This policy is designed to ensure that customers receive the products they ordered in the condition expected. If a mystery box arrives damaged or its contents are not as described, this guarantee allows you to file a claim. Amazon will then investigate the issue and may offer a refund or replacement. This policy provides a safety net, making it less risky to purchase items that come with an element of surprise.

Another essential policy is related to returns and refunds. Amazon generally offers a 30-day return window for most products, but the specifics can vary depending on the seller and the type of product. For mystery boxes, which often contain a variety of items, the return policy can be a bit more complex. Some sellers might offer partial refunds if only certain items in the box are unsatisfactory, while others may require the entire box to be returned. Reading the return policy before making a purchase can save you from potential headaches later on.

Amazon's Seller Performance Standards are also worth noting. These standards ensure that sellers maintain a high level of customer service, which includes timely shipping, accurate product descriptions, and responsive communication. Sellers who fail to meet these standards may face penalties, such as being banned from selling on the platform. For buyers, this means that a seller with high ratings and positive reviews is more likely to provide a satisfactory mystery box experience.

The platform also has specific guidelines about prohibited items. These guidelines ensure that certain products, such as hazardous materials or counterfeit goods, are not sold on Amazon. While it's unlikely that a mystery box would contain such items, being aware of these guidelines can help you identify and avoid potentially problematic sellers.

Payment policies are another crucial aspect to consider. Amazon accepts a variety of payment methods, including credit cards, debit cards, and gift cards. The platform also uses secure payment processing to protect your financial information. For those purchasing mystery boxes, using a secure payment method can provide additional peace of mind.

Lastly, it's important to understand the communication policies. Amazon encourages buyers and sellers to communicate through its messaging system, which is monitored to prevent fraud and abuse. If you have questions about a mystery box or encounter issues, using this system ensures that there is a record of all communications, which can be helpful if you need to escalate a dispute.

In essence, Amazon's policies are designed to create a safe and reliable shopping environment. By familiarizing yourself with these guidelines, you can navigate the world of mystery boxes with confidence, knowing that you are protected by a robust framework of rules and regulations.

ENSURING ETHICAL PRACTICES

As buyers, the allure of the unknown can be compelling, but it also brings with it a responsibility to ensure that our actions are grounded in ethical practices. When diving into this intriguing marketplace, it's vital to consider the broader implications of our purchasing decisions.

First and foremost, understanding the origin of these mystery boxes is crucial. Many sellers source their items from liquidation sales, returns, or overstocked inventory. While this can be a sustainable way to recycle goods that might otherwise go to waste, it is important to ensure that the sellers are transparent about the source and condition of the items within the box. Ethical buying starts with choosing sellers who provide honest descriptions and have a track record of fair dealing.

Moreover, the thrill of unboxing should not overshadow the necessity of supporting legitimate businesses. It's essential to avoid sellers who might be offloading stolen or counterfeit goods. Engaging in transactions with reputable vendors not only safeguards your investment but also supports a marketplace where ethical standards are upheld. Checking reviews, ratings, and seller feedback can help in identifying trustworthy sources.

Another critical aspect is the consideration of the environmental impact. The excitement of receiving a mystery box should be balanced with an awareness of the potential waste generated from unwanted items. Buyers should be prepared to responsibly manage any items they do not wish to keep. This can include donating, recycling, or reselling goods rather than discarding them. By doing so, we contribute to a more sustainable cycle of consumption.

Ethical practices also extend to how we handle our own expectations and reactions. The nature of mystery boxes means that not every purchase will yield high-value or desirable items. It's important to approach each box with a sense of adventure and a realistic mindset. Managing expectations helps in maintaining a positive experience and reduces the likelihood of impulsive or regretful purchasing behaviors.

Furthermore, consider the broader social implications of your purchases. Supporting small businesses and independent sellers who ethically source and sell their mystery boxes can have a positive impact on local economies and communities. This can also foster a more diverse and vibrant marketplace, where ethical practices are the norm rather than the exception.

In addition, engaging with the community of mystery box enthusiasts can provide valuable insights and support. Sharing experiences, tips, and recommendations not only enhances your own buying experience but also contributes to a culture of transparency and trust among buyers and sellers alike. Online forums, social media groups, and review platforms are excellent resources for this kind of interaction.

Lastly, it's beneficial to stay informed about any changes in regulations or policies related to online purchases and consumer rights. Being aware of your rights as a buyer ensures that you can make informed decisions and seek recourse if necessary. This knowledge empowers you to navigate the mystery box market with confidence and integrity.

In conclusion, ensuring ethical practices in the purchase of Amazon mystery boxes requires a mindful approach that considers the origins of the items, supports legitimate and transparent sellers, manages environmental impact, and fosters positive community engagement. By prioritizing these principles, you can enjoy the thrill of mystery boxes while contributing to a fair and sustainable marketplace.

HANDLING DISPUTES AND RETURNS

One of the more daunting aspects for buyers is addressing disputes and managing returns. When the thrill of the unknown turns into the frustration of the unexpected, knowing how to effectively handle these situations becomes essential.

Upon receiving a mystery box, the first step is to carefully inspect its contents. This initial inspection is crucial as it sets the foundation for any potential claims or disputes. Take clear, detailed photographs of the items as they are unpacked. Documenting the condition of the products not only serves as personal records but also becomes invaluable evidence if an issue arises.

When an item is found to be defective, damaged, or significantly not as described, it's important to act promptly. Amazon's return policy typically provides a limited window for returns and disputes, often within 30 days of receipt. The first course of action is to contact the seller directly through Amazon's messaging system. In your communication, be concise and polite, clearly stating the issue and providing the photographic evidence you gathered during your inspection.

Many sellers are willing to resolve issues amicably. They may offer a replacement, a refund, or a partial refund depending on the situation. It's beneficial to know your rights as a consumer; familiarizing yourself with Amazon's A-to-Z Guarantee can provide additional protection. This guarantee covers the timely delivery and condition of your items, offering a level of security when dealing with third-party sellers.

In instances where the seller is unresponsive or unwilling to resolve the issue satisfactorily, escalating the matter to Amazon's customer service is the next step. Utilize the "Get help with an order" option found in your order details. Amazon's customer service team can intervene, often providing refunds or facilitating returns when the seller fails to meet their obligations.

Returning items from a mystery box can sometimes be more complex than a standard return. Ensure that you follow Amazon's specific return instructions closely. This might include using a provided return label and packaging the items securely to prevent further damage during transit. Keep a record of your return tracking number as proof of shipment.

Patience and persistence are key during this process. While it can be frustrating, maintaining a calm and methodical approach increases the likelihood of a favorable resolution. Engaging with

Amazon's support through multiple channels—such as phone, chat, and email—can also expedite the process.

Avoiding disputes and returns in the first place is ideal. Researching sellers beforehand, reading reviews from other buyers, and understanding the specifics of the mystery box offerings can mitigate risks. Some sellers provide detailed descriptions and images of potential box contents, which can set more accurate expectations.

While the excitement of uncovering hidden treasures is the primary allure of Amazon mystery boxes, being prepared to handle disputes and returns ensures that the experience remains enjoyable. Equipping oneself with knowledge and tools to address issues effectively transforms potential setbacks into manageable situations, allowing the mystery and excitement to continue.

MAINTAINING TRANSPARENCY WITH BUYERS

When engaging in the intriguing world of Amazon mystery boxes, maintaining an open line of communication with buyers is paramount. Ensuring transparency can help build trust, foster repeat business, and create a loyal customer base. This subchapter delves into the various facets of maintaining transparency with buyers to elevate the buying experience and sustain long-term success.

The first step in fostering transparency is clear and accurate product descriptions. When listing a mystery box, it is essential to provide potential buyers with as much relevant information as possible without revealing the contents. This can include the type of items generally found in the boxes, their potential uses, and any specific themes or categories they might fall into. Providing this information helps manage buyer expectations and reduces the risk of disappointment upon receiving the box.

One effective way to enhance transparency is by sharing past buyer experiences. Encouraging previous customers to leave reviews and feedback can offer new buyers a glimpse into what they can expect. Highlighting both positive and constructive feedback demonstrates a commitment to honesty and gives potential buyers a well-rounded view of the product. Additionally, responding to reviews, whether they are positive or negative, shows that you value customer input and are dedicated to improving their experience.

Transparency also extends to the pricing of mystery boxes. Clearly outlining the cost, including any potential additional fees such as shipping or handling, ensures that buyers are fully aware of what they are paying for. It is important to avoid any hidden charges that could lead to buyer dissatisfaction. Offering a breakdown of costs, if applicable, can further instill confidence in the fairness of the pricing.

Another critical aspect is the condition of the items within the mystery boxes. While the nature of a mystery box is to provide an element of surprise, it is crucial to assure buyers that the items included are in good condition. If the box contains used or refurbished items, this should be clearly stated in the product description. Providing information about the quality and condition of the items can help set realistic expectations and prevent potential disputes.

Communication plays a vital role in maintaining transparency. Keeping buyers informed throughout the purchasing process, from order confirmation to shipping updates, can significantly enhance their experience. Providing detailed tracking information allows buyers to know exactly when to expect their mystery box, building anticipation and excitement. In case of any delays or issues, proactive communication can help manage expectations and maintain trust.

Offering a clear and fair return policy is another way to demonstrate transparency. Buyers should feel confident that if they are unsatisfied with their purchase, they have options available to them. Clearly outlining the return process, including any conditions or time frames, ensures that buyers are fully aware of their rights. A hassle-free return policy can also encourage more people to take the plunge and purchase a mystery box, knowing they have recourse if it does not meet their expectations.

Finally, maintaining transparency involves continuously seeking feedback and making improvements based on customer input. Regularly reviewing feedback and making necessary adjustments to the product or service can help address any recurring issues and enhance the overall buyer experience. Showing that you value and act upon customer feedback reinforces trust and demonstrates a commitment to providing the best possible service.

By prioritizing transparency in all aspects of the buying process, sellers can build a strong, trusting relationship with their customers. This not only enhances the immediate buying experience but also fosters long-term loyalty and success in the fascinating world of Amazon mystery boxes.

Chapter 10: Case Studies and Examples

SUCCESSFUL MYSTERY BOX PURCHASES

The thrill of anticipation begins to build the moment you click that purchase button. A sense of adventure tinged with a hint of the unknown makes buying an Amazon mystery box an exhilarating experience. Imagine a plain, nondescript cardboard box arriving at your doorstep, its contents concealed within layers of packaging. The weight of the box, the sound it makes when shaken gently, all add to the suspense.

Opening a mystery box is like unwrapping a gift from a friend who knows your quirks and interests. The first cut of the tape sends a shiver of excitement down your spine. As the flaps of the box open, your eyes dart to the first glimpse of the contents. You find yourself peeling back layers of bubble wrap and tissue paper, each layer revealing a new surprise.

The variety can be astonishing. Nestled among the packing materials, you might discover an assortment of items that range from the practical to the whimsical. A sleek wireless charger, perfect for your nightstand, sits next to a quirky ceramic mug adorned with a witty quote. Further exploration reveals a high-quality set of headphones and a beautifully illustrated notebook, each item sparking joy and curiosity.

What makes a mystery box purchase successful goes beyond the monetary value of the items. It's about the serendipity of discovering something you didn't know you needed or wanted. Perhaps you find a novel by an author you've never heard of, opening up a new world of literary adventures. Or maybe there's a kitchen gadget that simplifies your daily routine in ways you hadn't imagined.

The sensory experience is also a significant part of the allure. The tactile pleasure of unwrapping, the crinkle of paper, and the subtle scent of newness all contribute to the overall enjoyment. Each item tells a story, inviting you to imagine its journey from the warehouse to your home. The mystery box becomes a treasure trove, each object a piece of a larger puzzle.

Sometimes, the value of a mystery box lies in its ability to surprise you with items that hold sentimental value or evoke nostalgia. A vintage-style keychain might remind you of childhood summers at your grandparents' house. A set of artisanal coasters could transport you to a cozy café in a distant city, sparking memories of past travels.

It's also about the shared experience. Unboxing a mystery box with friends or family can turn an ordinary day into a celebration. Laughter, exclamations of delight, and the occasional puzzled look as you try to decipher the purpose of an unusual item all add to the fun. The collective excitement amplifies the joy, making the experience even more memorable.

In essence, a successful mystery box purchase is a blend of tangible and intangible elements. It's the perfect harmony of surprise, value, and personal connection. Each box is a unique adventure, offering a momentary escape from the routine and a chance to indulge in the simple pleasures of discovery.

LESSONS FROM UNSUCCESSFUL BUYS

Unveiling the allure of Amazon mystery boxes often feels like unlocking a treasure chest. The anticipation, the excitement, the sheer thrill of not knowing what lies within can be intoxicating. However, not every purchase leads to satisfaction. Some boxes, once opened, reveal items that fall short of expectations, leading to disappointment. These experiences, though disheartening, are invaluable for those who seek to master the art of buying Amazon mystery boxes.

One of the most crucial lessons learned from these unsuccessful buys is the importance of managing expectations. When the contents of a mystery box are revealed to be underwhelming, it often stems from inflated hopes. The mind conjures up images of high-value items, rare collectibles, or cutting-edge gadgets. Yet, the reality can be quite different. By approaching each box with a balanced mindset, the sting of disappointment can be mitigated. Understanding that not every box will contain a hidden gem helps in maintaining a level-headed perspective.

Another significant insight is the necessity of thorough research. While the essence of a mystery box is its unpredictability, there are often clues that can guide a more informed purchase. Reviews from previous buyers, seller ratings, and detailed descriptions can provide a glimpse into the potential contents and overall value. Ignoring these indicators can lead to regrettable buys. Learning to decode these hints enhances the ability to make better purchasing decisions, reducing the likelihood of encountering unsatisfactory boxes.

Budgeting plays a pivotal role in the realm of mystery boxes. The allure of potentially valuable items can tempt buyers to spend beyond their means. However, the unpredictability of the contents means that there is always a risk involved. Allocating a specific budget for mystery boxes and adhering to it ensures that financial stability is maintained, even if the box turns out to be less valuable than anticipated. This disciplined approach prevents the frustration that arises from overspending on disappointing items.

The experience of unsatisfactory buys also highlights the importance of resilience. It is easy to become disheartened after receiving a box filled with items that do not meet expectations. However, each unsuccessful purchase is a stepping stone towards better decision-making. Analyzing what went wrong, whether it was due to overlooked details or unrealistic expectations, equips buyers with the knowledge to avoid similar pitfalls in the future. This resilience transforms each setback into a valuable learning opportunity.

Moreover, it is essential to recognize the subjective nature of value. What may seem like a disappointing item to one person might be a treasure to another. Personal interests, needs, and preferences play a significant role in determining the worth of the contents. Keeping an open mind and appreciating the diversity of items can lead to unexpected satisfaction. This perspective shift turns the process into a more enjoyable and enriching experience.

Lastly, the community aspect should not be underestimated. Engaging with fellow mystery box enthusiasts provides a platform for sharing experiences, tips, and recommendations. Learning from others' successes and failures fosters a sense of camaraderie and collective wisdom. This network can be a valuable resource, offering insights that enhance the overall purchasing strategy.

In essence, the journey of buying Amazon mystery boxes is as much about the thrill of discovery as it is about learning from missteps. Each unsuccessful buy, while initially disheartening, contributes to a deeper understanding and appreciation of the process. Through managed expectations, thorough research, disciplined budgeting, resilience, subjective value recognition, and community engagement, the art of buying mystery boxes evolves into a more refined and rewarding pursuit.

ANALYZING DIFFERENT STRATEGIES

When it comes to purchasing Amazon mystery boxes, a variety of strategies can be employed to maximize the potential for exciting and valuable finds. Each approach has its own set of advantages and risks, making it crucial to understand the nuances that differentiate them.

One common strategy is to focus on seller ratings and reviews. By selecting sellers with high ratings and positive feedback, buyers can increase their chances of receiving quality items. This approach relies heavily on the experiences of previous customers, providing a sense of security and predictability. Buyers often scrutinize the number of reviews and the consistency of positive feedback, seeking sellers with a solid reputation. This method can be particularly effective for those new to the mystery box market, as it minimizes the risk of disappointment.

Another popular strategy involves targeting specific categories or themes. Mystery boxes can be curated around a wide range of interests, from electronics to collectibles, fashion to toys. By choosing boxes that align with personal interests or hobbies, buyers can enhance their satisfaction and enjoyment. This approach requires a bit of research to identify sellers who specialize in particular categories. Enthusiasts can find immense joy in discovering items that complement their existing collections or introduce them to new facets of their interests.

Price-based strategies also play a significant role in the mystery box buying process. Some buyers opt for higher-priced boxes, operating under the assumption that spending more will yield better-quality items. This high-risk, high-reward approach can lead to substantial gains but also comes with the potential for significant losses. Conversely, budget-conscious buyers might gravitate towards lower-cost boxes, appreciating the thrill of the hunt without a substantial financial commitment. This method can be particularly appealing to those who enjoy the element of surprise but are wary of potential financial pitfalls.

A more analytical strategy involves studying the contents of previously sold mystery boxes. Many sellers provide descriptions or photos of past boxes, offering valuable insights into the types of items typically included. By examining these records, buyers can gauge the likelihood of receiving desirable products and make more informed decisions. This data-driven approach appeals to those who prefer a more calculated risk, balancing the excitement of the unknown with a degree of predictability.

Networking and community engagement also contribute to effective mystery box purchasing strategies. Online forums, social media groups, and dedicated websites provide platforms for buyers to share experiences, tips, and recommendations. Engaging with these communities can reveal trustworthy sellers, uncover hidden gems, and provide support for navigating the complexities of the market. This collaborative approach fosters a sense of camaraderie among buyers, enhancing the overall experience and increasing the chances of success.

Some buyers employ a combination of strategies, blending elements of each to create a personalized approach. For instance, they might start by researching seller ratings and reviews, then narrow their focus to specific categories that interest them. They could set a budget that balances the potential for high-quality items with financial prudence, all while staying informed through community engagement. This multifaceted strategy allows for flexibility and adaptability, catering to the unique preferences and risk tolerance of the individual buyer.

In essence, the key to successfully purchasing Amazon mystery boxes lies in understanding the various strategies available and selecting the one that best aligns with personal goals and preferences. Whether prioritizing seller reputation, focusing on specific categories, considering price points, analyzing past box contents, or engaging with the community, each approach offers a unique path to uncovering the hidden treasures within these enigmatic packages.

LEARNING FROM OTHERS' EXPERIENCES

One of the most effective ways to mitigate the risks and enhance the rewards is by learning from the experiences of others who have ventured down this path. The collective wisdom of seasoned buyers can provide invaluable insights and practical tips, guiding newcomers through the maze of mystery box purchasing.

Engaging with online forums and communities dedicated to mystery box enthusiasts is a treasure trove of information. These platforms are filled with detailed reviews, unboxing videos, and candid discussions about the contents and value of various mystery boxes. By immersing oneself in these conversations, prospective buyers can gather a wealth of knowledge about which sellers are reputable, which boxes tend to offer the best value for money, and which ones to avoid.

It's not just about reading reviews; watching unboxing videos can be particularly enlightening. Seeing firsthand what others receive can set realistic expectations and help buyers understand the range of possibilities. Some unboxers offer detailed analyses of the items they receive, breaking down the potential resale value or personal utility of each item. This can be especially helpful for those who are considering purchasing mystery boxes with the intention of reselling the contents.

Another critical aspect of learning from others' experiences is paying attention to the red flags they highlight. Many experienced buyers share cautionary tales of boxes that were significantly delayed, contained damaged goods, or were filled with items of little to no value. These stories can serve as important warnings, helping new buyers to avoid similar pitfalls. Understanding common issues and knowing how to address them can make the difference between a satisfying purchase and a disappointing one.

In addition to learning from negative experiences, there is much to be gained from success stories. Some buyers have developed strategies for maximizing their chances of receiving high-value items. These strategies might include purchasing from specific sellers known for their generous boxes, timing purchases around certain sales or promotions, or even communicating directly with sellers to express preferences. By adopting these tactics, new buyers can improve their odds of a rewarding unboxing experience.

Social media platforms also play a significant role in the mystery box community. Hashtags, groups, and pages dedicated to this niche are abundant on sites like Instagram, Facebook, and Reddit. Following these accounts can provide a steady stream of updates, tips, and trends. Engaging with these communities not only keeps buyers informed but also connects them with like-minded individuals who share their enthusiasm and curiosity.

When delving into the world of Amazon mystery boxes, it's beneficial to approach each purchase with a blend of optimism and caution. The insights gained from others' experiences can serve as a roadmap, highlighting both the potential rewards and the possible pitfalls. Each unboxing is a learning opportunity, adding to the collective knowledge that makes the community so valuable.

By taking the time to research, watch, and listen, buyers can make more informed decisions, ultimately enhancing their experience with Amazon mystery boxes. The shared experiences of others act as a guiding light, illuminating the path for newcomers and helping them navigate the exciting, unpredictable world of mystery box purchasing.

Chapter 11: Future of Mystery Boxes

TRENDS IN THE MYSTERY BOX MARKET

Mystery boxes have captivated the curiosity of consumers, blending the thrill of the unknown with the potential for unexpected treasures. This phenomenon has seen a significant surge in recent years, particularly with the rise of e-commerce platforms like Amazon, which have made these enigmatic parcels more accessible than ever. The allure lies in the anticipation, the suspense of unwrapping a box that could contain anything from mundane household items to high-end electronics.

The popularity of mystery boxes can be traced back to several key trends. First, the unboxing experience itself has become a form of entertainment, amplified by social media influencers and YouTube personalities who share their discoveries with millions of followers. These unboxing videos often go viral, creating a ripple effect that drives more consumers to try their luck. The visual and emotional appeal of these videos cannot be understated; the shared excitement and reactions of the unboxers foster a sense of community and shared experience among viewers.

Another trend fueling the mystery box market is the shift towards experiential consumption. Modern consumers, particularly millennials and Gen Z, value experiences over material possessions. The act of purchasing and opening a mystery box is an experience in itself, providing a rush of adrenaline and a break from the predictability of everyday shopping. This trend aligns with the broader movement towards gamification in retail, where the shopping process is infused with elements of play and chance.

Economic factors also play a crucial role. Mystery boxes often promise high-value items at a fraction of their retail price, appealing to bargain hunters and those looking for a good deal. The potential to receive items worth significantly more than the purchase price creates a sense of perceived value that is hard to resist. This perception of value is further enhanced by the scarcity and exclusivity of certain items, which can only be obtained through these boxes.

The rise of subscription services has also contributed to the proliferation of mystery boxes. Monthly subscription boxes that deliver a curated selection of items have become a staple in many households. These boxes often tap into niche markets, offering everything from beauty products to gourmet snacks, and cater to specific interests and hobbies. The recurring nature of these subscriptions keeps consumers engaged and eagerly anticipating their next delivery.

Technological advancements have streamlined the process of purchasing and distributing mystery boxes. E-commerce platforms like Amazon have sophisticated algorithms that can curate and recommend boxes based on consumer preferences and purchasing history. This personalization enhances the appeal and relevance of the mystery box, making it more likely that the contents will align with the buyer's interests.

Environmental and ethical considerations are also emerging trends in the mystery box market. As consumers become more conscious of sustainability, there is a growing demand for eco-friendly packaging and responsibly sourced products. Some companies are responding by offering mystery boxes that are not only exciting but also environmentally responsible, using recyclable materials and including items that promote sustainable living.

In essence, the mystery box market is a dynamic and evolving landscape, driven by a confluence of social, economic, and technological factors. The excitement of the unknown, coupled with the potential for high-value rewards and the influence of digital media, continues to propel this trend forward. As consumers seek out new and engaging experiences, the mystery box phenomenon shows no signs of waning.

TECHNOLOGICAL INNOVATIONS

The landscape of e-commerce has been dramatically transformed by a series of technological innovations, each one enhancing the way consumers interact with platforms like Amazon. These advancements have redefined the shopping experience, turning it into a more dynamic and engaging activity. One such innovation is the use of sophisticated algorithms that personalize the shopping journey. Amazon's recommendation engine, for example, utilizes machine learning to analyze user behavior and preferences, suggesting products that are likely to capture interest. This technology not only aids consumers in discovering new items but also increases the likelihood of satisfaction with their purchases.

The integration of augmented reality (AR) has further revolutionized online shopping. With AR applications, customers can now visualize products in their intended environments before making a purchase. This technology is particularly beneficial for items such as furniture or home decor, where spatial compatibility is crucial. By allowing users to see how a couch might look in their living room or how a painting might fit on their wall, AR significantly reduces the uncertainty that often accompanies online purchases.

Blockchain technology has also started to make its mark, particularly in ensuring the authenticity and traceability of products. By providing a decentralized ledger that records every transaction, blockchain offers consumers increased transparency and trust. This is especially relevant for high-value items or products where provenance is important, such as collectibles or luxury goods. Knowing the history and journey of a product from its origin to delivery can reassure buyers and enhance their confidence in the platform.

Another noteworthy innovation is the development of voice-activated shopping. Devices like Amazon Echo and Google Home have made it possible for consumers to make purchases using simple voice commands. This hands-free approach is not only convenient but also inclusive, catering to individuals with disabilities or those who find traditional browsing cumbersome. The seamless integration of these devices with e-commerce platforms has added a new dimension to the shopping experience, making it more accessible and efficient.

The rise of big data analytics cannot be overlooked. By analyzing vast amounts of data, companies can gain insights into consumer behavior, preferences, and trends. This information is invaluable for tailoring marketing strategies and optimizing inventory management. For consumers, it means more relevant advertisements, better product recommendations, and timely promotions. Big data also plays a crucial role in identifying and mitigating potential risks, such as fraud or supply chain disruptions, ensuring a smoother and more secure shopping experience.

The proliferation of mobile technology has also had a profound impact. With the majority of consumers now using smartphones to shop online, mobile-optimized websites and apps have become essential. Features such as one-click purchasing, mobile wallets, and push notifications enhance the convenience and immediacy of mobile shopping. The ability to shop anytime and anywhere has made e-commerce more accessible than ever, catering to the fast-paced lifestyles of modern consumers.

Artificial intelligence (AI) chatbots have emerged as another game-changer, providing instant customer support and assistance. These AI-driven assistants can handle a wide range of queries, from tracking orders to resolving issues, offering 24/7 support. Their ability to learn and adapt over time ensures they provide increasingly accurate and helpful responses, enhancing overall customer satisfaction.

These technological innovations collectively contribute to a more personalized, efficient, and secure shopping experience. They have not only made e-commerce platforms like Amazon more user-friendly but have also opened up new possibilities for how consumers discover and purchase products.

PREDICTIONS FOR THE FUTURE

Peering into the horizon of the Amazon mystery box phenomenon reveals a landscape rich with potential and innovation. As e-commerce continues to evolve, the allure of the unknown will likely grow stronger, drawing even more enthusiasts into this intriguing world. The excitement of unwrapping a mystery box, filled with the anticipation of discovering hidden treasures, is a sensation that transcends age and demographic boundaries. This element of surprise taps into a deep-seated human desire for discovery and adventure.

The future of Amazon mystery boxes could see a proliferation of specialized categories, tailored to niche interests and hobbies. Imagine mystery boxes curated specifically for tech enthusiasts, filled with the latest gadgets and accessories, or for book lovers, containing rare editions and exclusive literary merchandise. This diversification can cater to a broader audience, making the experience even more personalized and enticing.

Technological advancements will likely play a pivotal role in shaping the future of this trend. Enhanced algorithms and AI could be employed to better match mystery box contents with buyer preferences, increasing satisfaction and reducing the risk of disappointment. Virtual reality (VR) and augmented reality (AR) might also be integrated, allowing customers to virtually "unwrap" their boxes before making a purchase, adding an extra layer of excitement and engagement.

Sustainability will become an increasingly important factor in the evolution of Amazon mystery boxes. As consumers grow more environmentally conscious, there will be a push for eco-friendly packaging and the inclusion of sustainable products. Companies might also adopt a circular economy model, where customers can return unwanted items for recycling or repurposing, thereby minimizing waste and promoting a more sustainable shopping experience.

The social aspect of mystery box buying is poised to expand as well. Online communities and social media platforms already play a significant role in this phenomenon, with unboxing videos and reviews generating substantial engagement. In the future, we might see the rise of dedicated mystery box influencers and content creators, whose recommendations and experiences will guide purchasing decisions. Live unboxing events, streamed in real-time, could become popular, turning what was once a solitary activity into a shared, communal experience.

E-commerce giants like Amazon may also introduce subscription-based mystery box services, offering customers a regular supply of curated surprises. This model could foster brand loyalty and provide a steady revenue stream, while continually captivating customers with the thrill of the unknown. Additionally, collaborations with popular brands and franchises could lead to exclusive, limited-edition mystery boxes, further elevating the appeal and exclusivity of the experience.

The intersection of commerce and entertainment will likely blur even further, as gamification elements are incorporated into the mystery box buying process. Customers might earn points or rewards for each purchase, unlocking additional surprises or discounts. Interactive challenges and scavenger hunts could be introduced, creating an immersive and engaging shopping adventure.

The future of Amazon mystery boxes is bright and multifaceted, driven by innovation, personalization, and a deep-rooted human love for mystery and exploration. As this trend continues to evolve, it will undoubtedly adapt to the changing preferences and values of consumers, ensuring that the thrill of unwrapping a mystery box remains as captivating as ever.

HOW TO STAY AHEAD OF THE CURVE

In the ever-evolving world of Amazon mystery boxes, the key to sustained success lies in the ability to anticipate and adapt to changes. The marketplace is a dynamic ecosystem, constantly shifting with trends, consumer preferences, and technological advancements. To maintain a competitive edge, one must be vigilant and proactive, always seeking out the latest information and innovations.

Staying informed about market trends is crucial. Subscribing to industry newsletters, following influential bloggers, and joining relevant social media groups can provide valuable insights. These sources often highlight emerging trends, popular products, and shifts in consumer behavior. By keeping a finger on the pulse of the market, one can make informed decisions that align with current demands.

Networking with other enthusiasts and professionals within the community can also be highly beneficial. Engaging in discussions, attending webinars, and participating in forums allows for the exchange of ideas and experiences. This collaborative approach not only broadens one's perspective but also opens up opportunities for partnerships and collaborations, further enhancing one's ability to stay ahead.

Technological advancements play a significant role in the mystery box landscape. Leveraging tools and software designed for market analysis, inventory management, and sales tracking can streamline operations and provide a competitive advantage. Utilizing data analytics to assess the performance of different boxes and identify profitable niches ensures that one remains agile and responsive to market changes.

Diversification is another strategy to consider. Relying solely on a single type of mystery box can be risky, especially if consumer interests shift. Exploring different categories, such as electronics, fashion, or home goods, can mitigate risks and tap into various market segments. It's important to remain flexible and open to experimenting with new products and box themes to discover what resonates with the audience.

Building strong relationships with suppliers is essential. Reliable suppliers can provide consistent quality and timely deliveries, which are critical for maintaining customer satisfaction. Establishing good communication channels and negotiating favorable terms can lead to better deals and exclusive access to high-demand products. A solid supplier network acts as a backbone, supporting the ability to adapt swiftly to market demands.

Customer feedback is an invaluable resource. Encouraging reviews and actively seeking feedback helps to understand the preferences and pain points of the audience. This direct line of communication allows for continuous improvement and customization of the offerings, ensuring that the boxes remain appealing and relevant.

Marketing strategies should also evolve with the times. Utilizing social media platforms, influencer partnerships, and targeted advertising can boost visibility and attract a broader audience. Staying updated with the latest marketing trends and tools enhances the ability to reach potential customers effectively.

Continuous learning and self-improvement are fundamental. Investing time in understanding new market strategies, attending workshops, and reading relevant literature can significantly enhance one's skills and knowledge. This commitment to personal growth translates into a more robust and adaptable approach to the mystery box business.

In essence, staying ahead in the Amazon mystery box arena requires a multifaceted approach. By keeping abreast of market trends, leveraging technology, diversifying products, fostering supplier relationships, valuing customer feedback, and adapting marketing strategies, one can navigate the complexities of the marketplace effectively. This proactive and informed approach ensures sustained success and resilience in the face of change.

Chapter 12: Personal Stories and Testimonials

FIRST-TIME BUYERS' EXPERIENCES

For many first-time buyers, the allure of Amazon mystery boxes is irresistible. The concept of receiving a package filled with unknown items sparks a sense of adventure and curiosity. Each box holds the promise of surprise, value, and the thrill of unboxing.

Imagine the excitement as the delivery truck pulls up to the house. The anticipation builds while the driver carries the box to the door. It's a moment charged with possibilities. The box, sealed and unassuming, sits waiting to reveal its secrets. The first-time buyer, armed with a pair of scissors or a box cutter, carefully slices through the tape, their heart pounding with expectation.

As the flaps of the box open, the first glimpse inside can be either exhilarating or perplexing. Some buyers find themselves greeted by a jumble of items, each one a potential treasure. There might be a brand-new gadget still in its packaging, a quirky decorative item, or even a high-end beauty product. The variety is often astonishing, and the diversity of the contents can make the experience feel like a mini treasure hunt right in the living room.

The first item pulled from the box might be something practical, like a set of kitchen utensils or a handy phone charger. It's not just the value that excites but also the utility. For some, it feels like hitting the jackpot, finding something they needed but didn't expect. Each subsequent item adds to the narrative of the unboxing, creating a story with every layer peeled back.

However, the experience isn't always perfect. There can be moments of disappointment when an item is damaged or not as exciting as hoped. A first-time buyer might pull out a piece of clothing that's not their size or style, or a tech accessory for a device they don't own. Yet, even these moments add to the overall adventure. They become part of the story, a chapter in the journey of discovering what lies within the box.

For some, the first-time experience is marked by a learning curve. They begin to understand the nuances of selecting the right seller, the importance of reading reviews, and the value of setting realistic expectations. It's a process of trial and error, but one that often leads to refined strategies for future purchases.

Community and shared experiences play a significant role for many first-time buyers. Online forums and social media groups are filled with stories, tips, and photos of unboxed treasures. These platforms become a space for celebrating great finds and commiserating over less-than-stellar items. The shared excitement and advice from more seasoned buyers can transform the experience from a solitary activity into a communal event.

In the end, the thrill of the unknown is what captivates first-time buyers. The blend of anticipation, discovery, and the occasional surprise makes each box an adventure. It's not just about the items themselves, but the journey of finding them, the stories they create, and the connections they foster. This blend of mystery and excitement is what keeps many coming back, eager to open the next box and see what wonders it holds.

SEASONED BUYERS' INSIGHTS

In the dimly lit corners of the internet, where the allure of the unknown beckons, seasoned buyers of Amazon mystery boxes have honed their craft. These veterans of the trade possess an almost mystical knack for discerning the treasures hidden within the nondescript cardboard confines. Their insights, gathered from countless purchases and unboxings, illuminate the path for the uninitiated.

In the world of mystery boxes, patience is a virtue. Experienced buyers advise against the impulsive click, urging instead a careful examination of the seller's reputation. Reviews and ratings are the breadcrumbs that lead to trustworthy sources. A seller with a consistent history of positive feedback often indicates a higher likelihood of receiving a box filled with items of genuine value. The seasoned buyer knows that a bit of research can make the difference between delight and disappointment.

The seasoned buyer also understands the importance of setting realistic expectations. They approach each box with a sense of curiosity rather than a hope for high-value items. Their joy is found in the thrill of discovery, the process of unwrapping each item and speculating on its origins and potential uses. This mindset transforms the act of unboxing into an experience that is enjoyable regardless of the monetary worth of the contents.

One key insight from these veterans is the art of diversification. They rarely put all their eggs in one basket, preferring instead to purchase from a variety of sellers and categories. This method not only increases the chances of stumbling upon a rare gem but also adds layers of excitement to the unboxing process. Each box becomes a unique story, a chapter in an ever-evolving narrative of exploration.

Storage auctions and liquidation sales are often the hunting grounds for these savvy buyers. They understand that mystery boxes originating from such sources can be a mixed bag, with items ranging from the mundane to the extraordinary. The seasoned buyer is adept at navigating these waters, recognizing the subtle signs that hint at a box's potential. They know that sometimes, the most unassuming packages can hold the greatest surprises.

Another lesson from the veterans is the importance of community. Forums, social media groups, and online marketplaces are invaluable resources where buyers share their experiences, offer recommendations, and warn against dubious sellers. Engaging with these communities provides a wealth of knowledge and can lead to more informed purchasing decisions. The seasoned buyer is never truly alone in their quest; they are part of a larger, interconnected network of enthusiasts and experts.

The seasoned buyer also pays close attention to the fine print. Terms and conditions, return policies, and shipping details are scrutinized with a keen eye. They know that understanding these nuances can prevent potential pitfalls and ensure a smoother transaction process. This meticulous approach reflects their commitment to making the most out of each purchase.

Through their experiences, seasoned buyers have developed a sixth sense for spotting hidden value. They can identify items that, while seemingly ordinary, possess a unique charm or utility. Their homes are filled with eclectic finds, each with a story to tell and a purpose to serve. This knack for uncovering hidden gems is a testament to their refined sensibilities and deep appreciation for the art of unboxing.

In the end, the insights of seasoned buyers offer a roadmap for navigating the world of Amazon mystery boxes. Their wisdom, born from countless unboxings and a genuine passion for discovery, serves as a guiding light for anyone willing to delve into this intriguing and unpredictable marketplace.

TRANSFORMATIVE FINDS

Each box, with its unassuming exterior, holds the promise of hidden treasures and transformative discoveries that can reshape perceptions and stir the imagination. As the seal breaks and the flaps unfold, a world of possibilities comes to life, offering not just products, but stories waiting to be told.

The first glimpse inside can be likened to the moment before dawn, where the darkness begins to yield to light, revealing shapes and forms that were previously concealed. The contents, often a mix of the familiar and the unknown, create an immediate sense of curiosity. An item as mundane as a kitchen gadget can become a source of fascination when it arrives unexpectedly. The mind races, considering its utility, its origin, and the serendipity that brought it into your possession.

Among the assortment, there are often pieces that stand out, not for their monetary value, but for the way they resonate on a personal level. A vintage book, its pages yellowed with age, may carry the scent of nostalgia, evoking memories of childhood stories and long-forgotten afternoons spent reading. Such finds have the power to transport one to different times and places, offering a glimpse into the lives of others and the history they carry.

In some boxes, there are items that spark creativity and innovation. Craft supplies, art materials, or even unusual tools can ignite a passion for new hobbies or rekindle old ones. A set of paints and brushes might inspire a budding artist to create a masterpiece, while a collection of beads and threads could lead to the crafting of unique jewelry pieces. These items, though seemingly insignificant at first, hold the potential to unlock hidden talents and foster a sense of accomplishment.

Moreover, the unexpected nature of these finds often leads to moments of genuine joy and surprise. A high-end gadget or a rare collectible can elicit a sense of triumph and excitement, transforming an ordinary day into an extraordinary one. The thrill of uncovering such treasures is akin to finding a hidden gem in a vast expanse, offering a tangible reward for the risk taken in purchasing the mystery box.

The transformative power of these finds extends beyond the physical objects themselves. They encourage a mindset of openness and adaptability, teaching the value of embracing the unknown and finding joy in unpredictability. Each box serves as a reminder that life, much like the contents within, is full of surprises, and that the greatest rewards often come from the least expected places.

In essence, the allure of Amazon mystery boxes lies not just in the items they contain, but in the experiences they offer. They challenge the conventional ways of shopping and gift-giving, turning the act of purchasing into an adventure. The discoveries made within these boxes can inspire, delight, and transform, making each unboxing a unique and unforgettable experience.

ADVICE FROM THE COMMUNITY

The allure of Amazon mystery boxes has captivated the minds of countless enthusiasts, each eager to unveil hidden treasures within unassuming cardboard confines. Among this burgeoning community, a collective wisdom has emerged, forged through countless unboxings and shared experiences. These seasoned explorers offer invaluable advice, a beacon for those venturing into the enigmatic world of Amazon mystery boxes.

Engaging with the community reveals a treasure trove of insights, starting with the importance of research. Veterans emphasize the necessity of scrutinizing sellers meticulously. Reputable sellers often have a history of positive reviews and transparent practices. Scouring forums, social media groups, and review sites can unearth gems of information, guiding buyers toward trustworthy sources and away from potential pitfalls.

A recurring theme in the community is the art of managing expectations. Experienced buyers caution against harboring dreams of striking gold in every box. The thrill, they say, lies in the unpredictability and the joy of discovery, rather than the monetary value of the contents. Embracing this mindset transforms the experience into a delightful adventure, where each item, regardless of its worth, holds a unique story.

Budgeting is another critical piece of advice echoed by many. Setting a clear, realistic budget prevents the excitement from spiraling into financial strain. Enthusiasts often share their budgeting strategies, recommending a balance between indulgence and prudence. This approach ensures that the thrill of the hunt remains a joyous pastime rather than a burden.

The community also underscores the significance of understanding the types of mystery boxes available. Some boxes are themed, focusing on specific categories like electronics, toys, or household items. Others are more eclectic, offering a mix of products. Seasoned buyers suggest aligning box choices with personal interests or needs, enhancing the likelihood of satisfaction with the contents.

Packaging and shipping nuances are frequently discussed topics. Experienced buyers share tips on recognizing well-packaged boxes, which often indicate a seller's attention to detail and care. They advise paying attention to shipping times and costs, as these can vary significantly and impact the overall value of the purchase.

The collective wisdom also highlights the importance of patience. The thrill of instant gratification is tempered by the understanding that some of the best finds come to those who wait. Whether it's waiting for the perfect box to appear or patiently sifting through its contents, patience is a virtue that seasoned buyers have learned to cultivate.

Unboxing techniques and rituals are another fascinating aspect shared within the community. Some prefer a meticulous, item-by-item reveal, savoring each discovery. Others opt for a more spontaneous approach, diving into the box with gleeful abandon. These shared rituals not only enhance the experience but also foster a sense of camaraderie among enthusiasts.

The community's advice often extends beyond the unboxing, touching on the creative ways to repurpose or enjoy the items found. Whether it's re-gifting, crafting, or incorporating the items into everyday life, these suggestions add an extra layer of value and enjoyment to the experience.

Engaging with fellow enthusiasts transforms the solitary act of unboxing into a shared adventure. The exchange of stories, tips, and discoveries builds a vibrant tapestry of collective knowledge, enriching the experience for all. The wisdom of the community serves as a guiding light, illuminating the path for both novices and seasoned explorers alike, ensuring that each journey into the world of Amazon mystery boxes is filled with wonder and delight.

Chapter 13: Conclusion and Next Steps

RECAP OF KEY POINTS

In the realm of e-commerce, one of the most intriguing and adventurous experiences a shopper can have is purchasing an Amazon Mystery Box. These enigmatic parcels, wrapped in an aura of suspense, promise a variety of surprises that can range from delightfully unexpected to whimsically bizarre. For the uninitiated, understanding the nuances of buying these mystery boxes can be a daunting task. However, delving into the key points can provide a clearer picture and enhance the overall experience.

Firstly, it's essential to grasp what an Amazon Mystery Box entails. Essentially, these are packages sold by various vendors on Amazon, filled with a random assortment of items. The contents can vary widely, encompassing anything from electronics, household goods, and toys, to more niche products like collectibles or fashion accessories. The allure lies in the unpredictability, the excitement of not knowing exactly what you will receive until you open the box.

One of the primary considerations when buying an Amazon Mystery Box is the reputation of the seller. Since these boxes are curated by third-party vendors, it is crucial to scrutinize seller ratings and reviews. A high rating and positive feedback from previous buyers can serve as indicators of reliability and quality. Conversely, a seller with numerous negative reviews might be a red flag, suggesting that the contents of their boxes may not meet your expectations.

Price is another significant factor. Amazon Mystery Boxes come in a wide range of price points, and it's important to set a budget beforehand. While it might be tempting to go for the cheapest option, remember that the value and quality of the items inside often correlate with the price. Investing a little more can sometimes yield a more satisfying assortment of products. However, it's also worth noting that higher-priced boxes do not always guarantee better contents, so balancing your budget with careful research is key.

Understanding the theme of the mystery box is also crucial. Some boxes are themed around specific categories, such as tech gadgets, beauty products, or children's toys. Selecting a theme that aligns with your interests or needs can increase the likelihood of receiving items that you will find useful or enjoyable. Reading the product description and any available reviews can provide insights into the likely contents and help you make an informed choice.

Shipping and return policies are additional aspects to consider. Since the contents are unknown, there is a possibility that you may receive items that are damaged or not to your liking. Checking the seller's return policy beforehand can save you from potential disappointment. Some sellers offer returns or exchanges, while others have a no-return policy, which means you would have to keep whatever you receive, regardless of its condition or utility.

Lastly, the element of fun and surprise should not be underestimated. While practical considerations are important, the primary appeal of an Amazon Mystery Box lies in the thrill of discovery. Approaching the purchase with an open mind and a sense of adventure can enhance the experience. It's about embracing the unexpected and enjoying the process of unveiling the mystery, much like unwrapping a gift.

In essence, buying an Amazon Mystery Box is a blend of strategic decision-making and playful curiosity. By paying attention to seller reputation, pricing, themes, and policies, while also indulging in the excitement of the unknown, you can navigate this unique shopping experience with confidence and joy.

SETTING FUTURE GOALS

Setting clear and achievable goals is essential when delving into the world of Amazon mystery boxes. The allure of these boxes lies in their unpredictability, but to make the most out of the experience, having a roadmap can significantly enhance your journey. Start by identifying your primary motivation for purchasing these mystery boxes. Are you seeking valuable items to resell, unique collectibles to add to your personal collection, or simply the thrill of the unknown? Clarifying your purpose will help guide your choices and expectations.

Next, consider setting a budget. The excitement of mystery boxes can sometimes lead to overspending, so it's crucial to establish a financial limit. Decide how much you're willing to invest in this venture and stick to it. This not only prevents financial strain but also allows you to measure the returns on your investment more accurately. Researching the average cost of mystery boxes and comparing them against your budget can provide a realistic framework for your spending.

Once your budget is in place, think about the frequency of your purchases. Will you buy a mystery box every month, every quarter, or just occasionally? Setting a timeline for your purchases can help manage your anticipation and provide a structured approach to your buying habits. This also allows you to track the outcomes of each box over time and adjust your strategy if needed.

It's also beneficial to set specific goals for the types of items you hope to find. While the contents of mystery boxes are unpredictable, having a wishlist can add to the excitement and satisfaction when you discover something that aligns with your desires. Whether it's rare collectibles, high-value electronics, or unique items that spark joy, having a mental (or physical) checklist can make the unboxing experience more rewarding.

Networking with other mystery box enthusiasts can also be a valuable goal. Engaging with a community of like-minded individuals can provide insights, tips, and even opportunities for trading items. Online forums, social media groups, and local meetups are excellent places to connect with others who share your interest. These interactions can enhance your understanding of the market, introduce you to reputable sellers, and offer a platform to share your experiences.

Documenting your unboxing experiences is another goal worth considering. Keeping a record of the items you receive, their estimated value, and your overall satisfaction can help you refine your future purchases. This documentation can be in the form of a journal, a spreadsheet, or even a blog or YouTube channel if you wish to share your adventures with a broader audience. Over time, this record can reveal patterns and help you make more informed decisions.

Lastly, remain adaptable and open to change. The world of Amazon mystery boxes is dynamic, and what works today might not yield the same results tomorrow. Regularly reviewing and adjusting your goals ensures that you stay aligned with your motivations and continue to enjoy the process. Flexibility allows you to pivot your approach based on new information, trends, and personal experiences, keeping the excitement alive and the outcomes favorable.

By setting thoughtful and strategic goals, you can transform the whimsical nature of Amazon mystery boxes into a structured and fulfilling endeavor.

CONTINUING YOUR JOURNEY

As you delve deeper into the world of Amazon mystery boxes, the excitement only intensifies. Each box, a sealed promise of treasures unknown, beckons with an allure that is hard to resist. The thrill of unwrapping these packages is akin to opening a time capsule, where the contents hold stories and potential far beyond their immediate appearance.

The first step in advancing your exploration is to refine your search techniques. Amazon's vast marketplace can be overwhelming, but with a few strategic approaches, you can navigate it with precision. Keywords are your allies in this quest. Instead of generic terms, opt for specific phrases that align with your interests. For instance, if you have a penchant for electronics, terms like "tech mystery box" or "gadget grab bag" can yield more relevant results. Reviews and ratings are invaluable tools. They offer insights into the experiences of previous buyers, guiding you towards reputable sellers and away from potential disappointments.

Another layer to consider is the seller's profile. A quick glance at their rating, feedback, and history can reveal much about their reliability. Engaging with sellers through questions can also be enlightening. Inquiring about the types of items typically included, return policies, and shipping details can provide clarity and set realistic expectations.

Diversifying your sources is another strategy worth exploring. While Amazon is a treasure trove, other platforms and independent sellers may offer unique mystery boxes that cater to niche interests. Websites like eBay, Etsy, and specialized subscription services have their own versions of these enigmatic packages. Each platform brings its own flavor, expanding the horizons of your discovery.

As you progress, it's beneficial to develop a system for managing your acquisitions. Cataloging items as they arrive can help track your collection and assess the value of each box. Whether through a digital spreadsheet or a physical journal, noting down the details—such as the box's theme, the items inside, and your overall satisfaction—can enhance your experience and inform future purchases.

Sharing your findings with a community can amplify the joy of this pursuit. Online forums, social media groups, and dedicated websites are bustling with fellow enthusiasts eager to exchange insights, tips, and even trade items. Engaging with these communities not only enriches your knowledge but also fosters connections with like-minded individuals who share your passion.

Budgeting is another crucial aspect to consider. The allure of mystery boxes can be intoxicating, but maintaining a balance between indulgence and financial prudence is key. Setting a monthly or quarterly budget ensures that your hobby remains sustainable and enjoyable over the long term.

Incorporating an element of creativity can transform your mystery box experience into a more personalized adventure. Customizing the way you unbox items, perhaps through themed unboxing parties or creating content to share online, can add layers of fun and engagement. Documenting these moments, whether through photos, videos, or written reviews, creates a tangible record of your journey, allowing you to revisit the thrill of each discovery.

As you continue to explore, remember that each mystery box is more than just a collection of items. It's an opportunity to uncover hidden gems, embrace surprises, and experience the joy of discovery. With each box, you peel back another layer of the unknown, enriching your understanding and appreciation of the myriad possibilities that lie within.

FINAL THOUGHTS

The journey of navigating the world of Amazon mystery boxes is akin to a treasure hunt, each box a chest waiting to be unlocked. As you stand at the threshold of this unique shopping experience, a plethora of possibilities stretches out before you. The anticipation and excitement that accompany the unboxing of these mystery boxes are unmatched, offering a blend of curiosity and thrill that few other purchases can provide.

Imagine the weight of the box in your hands, the tape still intact, holding within it the promise of discovery. The tactile sensation of cutting through the packing tape, the first glimpse of the contents beneath the flaps, and the rustling of packaging materials all add to the sensory delight. Each item you pull out tells a story, some familiar, others surprising. Perhaps you find a gadget you've always wanted or a quirky item you never knew existed but now cherish. The randomness of the contents ensures that no two experiences are alike, keeping the excitement alive with every box.

As you delve deeper into this world, you become more adept at discerning which boxes might hold the greatest potential. The subtle clues in the seller's descriptions, the weight and size of the box, and even the shipping origin start to form a pattern in your mind. This newfound skill transforms the act of purchasing into a strategic endeavor, where each decision is informed by your growing expertise.

The community of fellow mystery box enthusiasts adds another layer to the experience. Sharing your finds, discussing the best sellers, and even swapping items create a sense of camaraderie. The collective knowledge of this community can be invaluable, offering tips and insights that enhance your own adventures. Whether it's through online forums, social media groups, or in-person meetups, the connections you make enrich the overall experience.

There's also a practical side to consider. The potential for reselling items you don't need or want can turn this hobby into a profitable venture. Online marketplaces and local classifieds become venues where you can pass on your surplus finds to others, recouping some of your investment and making room for the next box. This cycle of buying, discovering, and reselling can be both financially beneficial and immensely satisfying.

However, it's essential to approach this hobby with a sense of balance. The allure of the unknown can sometimes lead to impulsive decisions, resulting in boxes that don't meet your expectations. Setting a budget and adhering to it ensures that the thrill of the hunt doesn't overshadow financial prudence.

Additionally, being mindful of the environmental impact of excessive purchasing and packaging waste encourages more sustainable practices.

Overall, the world of Amazon mystery boxes offers a unique blend of excitement, discovery, and community. Each box is a microcosm of potential, a small adventure waiting to unfold. The skills you develop, the connections you make, and the joy of uncovering unexpected treasures all contribute to a rich and rewarding experience. As you continue to explore this fascinating realm, remember to savor each moment, for it is the thrill of the unknown that makes this journey truly special.

Made in United States
North Haven, CT
04 May 2025

68549763R00088